THE SPORTSMAN AND HIS
FAMILY OUTDOORS

THE SPORTSMAN AND HIS FAMILY OUTDOORS

by Grits Gresham

Outdoor Life • E. P. Dutton & Co.
New York

Manufactured in the United States of America

CONTENTS

Introduction

FOR YEARS sportsmen have faced the dilemma of going off to hunt or fish without causing discontent on the home front. Resentment and bitterness have sometimes been the result of such "abandonment." But in recent years, many a wife has discovered that there are varied pleasures to be found afield, and is ready to pack her duffel bag when her husband heads for woods and streams. This eliminates the unpleasantness of leaving her behind, but . . .

How can a hunter or fisherman care for his wife and/or children in the outdoors, keep them happy and interested and safe, without sacrificing the pursuit and enjoyment of his own favorite outdoor activities? There are many ways, and this book will offer solutions to these problems, revealing happy alternatives to otherwise unpleasant situations.

Those alternatives are available, but the sportsman must reorient his thinking in order to use them. Wives and children may find pleasure in the sports of hunting and fishing, but there are many other activities associated with the outdoors which will take up the slack in case they don't. Sportsmen must become aware of them as means to keep the family occupied in the outdoors. In doing so they'll usually reap the additional benefit of discovering that they, too, find enjoyment in these related pursuits.

This decade, the sixties, should go down in history as the era when it became fashionable to enjoy the outdoors. For many years prior to this, tens of thousands of sportsmen and conservationists had been extolling the virtues and benefits and pleasures of outdoor activities, but for the most part their words fell only on the ears of other converts.

Suddenly, or so it seemed, the rush was on to the out-of-doors. The number of hunting and fishing licenses sold annually soared. So did the number of boats and motors which moved onto lake and stream, and the number of tents which were erected in campgrounds throughout the land. The pickup camper has become unbelievably popular, as has the tent trailer—the compromise between the rugged living of the pure tent and the luxury of the camper or trailer.

2

The crush of people bent on outdoor pleasure overwhelmed recreational facilities in many parts of the nation. Campgrounds were filled to overflow and the demand for more accommodations, and better accommodations, became louder and louder.

Federal, state and private agencies moved quickly to fill the obvious need for expanded programs keyed to the outdoors. Congress created the Bureau of Outdoor Recreation, and the Land and Water Conservation Act, which provides money for its operation. Older agencies of the federal government, including the Bureau of Sport Fisheries and Wildlife, the U. S. Department of Agriculture, the Soil Conservation Service and the U. S. Corps of Engineers, revamped their operations to keep in tune with growing public outdoor activities.

Outdoor enthusiasts who, for decades, had waged an unrelenting and lonesome fight against the unwise and unnecessary encroachment of civilization upon the outdoor resources of the nation, suddenly discovered support for their causes in all directions. No longer were there voices crying in the wilderness against water pollution, inroads into parks and wilderness areas, the evil of pesticides, the destruction of irreplaceable natural resources.

This new, welcomed support came from the masses and from key people in influential positions of government. When teamed with experienced individuals who had waged the battle for so long, this support generated enough momentum to create a Wild and Scenic Rivers System, to create a Redwood National Park, to activate a vigorous federal policy on water-pollution control, to pass a National Trails System Act, to create a system of Wilderness Areas, to establish a National Water Commission to conduct a comprehensive review of national water-resource problems and programs, to authorize an inventory and study of the nation's estuaries and their natural resources, and to create such a public awareness of the value of outdoor resources that few proposed projects which might damage them will escape detailed scrutiny and evaluation.

To the conservationist, professional or amateur, these achievements were the exciting fruits of years of effort. At last a groundswell of public opinion had been generated in favor of saving the remaining natural resources with which the nation is blessed, and of restoring areas amenable to such treatment.

To the sportsman, however, the sixties had additional meaning. These were the years when wives and children discovered the pleasures of the outdoors. The attention given to outdoor recreation and natural resources aroused the interest of millions.

This book is intended to serve as a guide for you, the sportsman, to help you recognize the opportunities which will satisfy this new desire of many wives and children to participate with you in your outdoor activities.

From the beginning, try to instill into the members of your family a love and respect for the outdoors. Our great natural environment needs all the help and support which can be mustered, and as our population grows that need will become more acute.

Environmental pollution from man's activities has already spread throughout the globe, even to the remotest regions, and a dedicated movement to reverse the process must be one of our major goals in the immediate years ahead. The advances in the technology of industrial production, and the formulation of chemical compounds to fight plant and animal pests, have outstripped our ability and/or willingness to treat the waste products properly and to use the pesticides intelligently.

Teach your family not to despoil the outdoors with litter. Make it a practice to leave the scene at least as nice as it was when you found it. Burn and bury your debris, or take it back home for disposal. There is great satisfaction in leaving a primitive campsite so clean and unspoiled that the next visitor has difficulty recognizing that a camper passed that way.

Keep in mind that sportsmen enjoy many facets of nature in a subconscious way. Hunters and fishermen recognize and appreciate the sights, sounds and smells of woods and streams without making an effort to do so. Time and experience have honed their senses of smell, sight, hearing and touch to a fine degree not often found in wives and youngsters who have never been exposed to the outdoors.

Make "patience" and "encouragement" your keynotes when you begin to take your wife and children afield with you. Your outdoor hobbies are fun for you, and they'll be fun for your family if you follow that rule.

Your teaching will overlap from one activity to another, just as the suggestions and ideas in the chapters of this book overlap. Learning to see the dimple of a feeding trout helps a student to be more alert to recognize an unusual bird species. Practice in listening for and identifying the song of a warbler is excellent training for hunting—for hearing the sound of squirrel claws on the bark of an oak tree. The proper clothes for a fall walk in the woods are usually ideal for fall fishing, hunting or camping.

The possibilities for enjoying the outdoors are obviously not confined to hunting and fishing, and the chapters of this book will explore some of these possibilities in detail. The ideas, if put to use, can enable all sportsmen to have their cake and eat it, too; to fully enjoy their own activities while taking their family along.

1 Hunting

How DOES a couple who loves hunting, and has no baby-sitter available, find happiness with a 4-year-old daughter and a 2-month-old son? Mary and I found ourselves in just that kind of situation when we lived in Arizona, and the way we coped with it is indicative of what can be accomplished if the desire is there.

On many occasions we spent several pleasant hours afield in the desert near Phoenix, and usually ended the day with a mixed bag of quail, cottontails and jack rabbits. Here's the way we did it.

We looked for a protected arroyo which was convenient to a back road, and set up housekeeping there. Housekeeping, in this case, meant a playpen for the baby, a Coleman stove on which to heat the baby's bottle and soup for the rest of the family, all near a sandy area in the dry wash where daughter Barbara could play.

We took turns hunting. One of us would mind the shop while the other hunted for an hour or so. Arroyos are concentration points for quail and cottontails, so we usually hunted up and down the one on which we were located.

There were certain precautions to be observed. I checked the area thoroughly to make sure it was free of animal or vegetable matter which might be unpleasant, such as snakes or ants or cactus. Mary and I each carried a whistle for signaling in an emergency, a contingency which we never experienced. We also worked out a signaling arrangement of shots for the same purpose, which also remained unused.

We took along a blanket to use as a windbreak around the playpen—a plastic sheet proved too noisy—and another one for the top when it was nap time. Toys and books went into our hunting package on these occasions, to be used by the appropriate members of the family. We improved and refined the operation as we went along, the overall results being most satisfactory.

This experience illustrates the two general situations faced by the sportsman who has a family, and who is reluctant to go afield and "abandon" his wife and/or children at home. The first situation is where the family members really want to join you in hunting or fishing or whatever your outdoor hobby happens to be. The other is the situation where they are not particularly interested in participating, but still don't want to be left behind all the time.

If your wife is already a hunter at the time you marry, you are fortunate to have a hunting partner. Most of the time, however, this is not the case. Then you are faced with the choice of whether or not to try to interest her in hunting, and if the answer is yes, how to proceed.

WIVES AND GUNS

It is important that every wife of a hunter becomes familiar with guns. Not only will she be around them in the house, but her attitude toward firearms and hunting will have its effect on the children. These would be sufficient reasons for encouraging a wife to join her husband in hunting activities, even if only on a minor scale, quite apart from the very real pleasure which husbands can experience through having their wives enjoy their sport.

Safety must be the overriding consideration in all aspects of hunting, shooting, gun handling and shooting instruction; indeed, in anything involving guns. Wives who have never been around firearms frequently have an unreasoning fear and dislike for them. This is the first obstacle which the husband must help her overcome.

Start by explaining that a gun is an inanimate object. As long as it remains untouched by people, it will just remain in its niche in the gun rack and bother nobody.

Stress that it is the misuse and mishandling of firearms that can make them dangerous. And stress that it is this same carelessness and irresponsibility which causes some 55,000 deaths in auto accidents each year.

What you are doing with your wife is to instill in her the kind of attitude you want her to transfer to your children. It's the right attitude, the reasonable attitude, and the only kind compatible in a household where the husband is an avid hunter.

The best time and place to begin your safety instruction is during your first shooting session. You want the experience to be fun as well as valuable, and this is easy to accomplish.

TRAINING WITH A BB GUN

Begin with a spring-powered BB gun—a Daisy, if you please. Most of us received our start in shooting in this fashion, and there is still no better way. The Daisy is ideal because noise and recoil are almost nonexistent, the range is limited, and the cost of shooting is negligible.

Recoil and report are the big bugaboos of beginning shooters. They fear the "kick" and the loud sound of a gunshot. After a few sessions with the BB rifle, most forget these hangups.

Insist that the Daisy be handled with the same degree of respect and safety which is required of more powerful guns. Here is where you build into your family the safe gun-handling traits which will become instinctive as time goes by, which will make them safe and enjoyable shooting companions.

Select a safe location for your shooting instruction, and here is where the BB rifle has another advantage. In many situations you'll find that your backyard is suitable for shooting an air rifle. If this is true, then it means that you can have frequent shooting sessions with little effort. This is important, since more sessions of short duration are preferable to a few long ones.

Teach beginners to shoot with both eyes open, using their stronger eye for sighting. If a right-handed person shoots best with his left eye, teach him to shoot left-handed, as the author is doing here with his son.

Don't overdo the training periods! This is something the avid hunter is apt to do without knowing it. Keep those first ones short and fun.

My first rule of gun safety is: Never point a gun at anybody or at anything you do not want to shoot. This is elementary, but a simple rule which would prevent *all* gun accidents if it were always followed. Exaggerate this precaution in your training sessions, and make it a point to correct your wife each time she forgets. The key word in the rule is "never," which means loaded or unloaded.

Even veteran hunters are frequently guilty of swinging the muzzle of a gun past a fellow hunter, and such a momentary lapse can be fatal. Insist on strict compliance with this cardinal rule of gun safety.

Treat every gun as if it were loaded. In my family we have developed a practice of checking each gun that comes into our hands by opening the action, to see whether it's loaded or not. If I pick up a gun I check it, yet when I hand it to one of my sons he checks it again. Don't take anybody's word for this important fact.

Shooting with a BB rifle at drifting objects on a lake or stream is good target practice. The splash of the BB in the water allows the shooter to call his shots. Do not shoot at water with more powerful rifles; the bullet can ricochet and injure someone.

It is rare to find an adult or child who doesn't know the principle of sighting a rifle—putting the blade front sight in the notch of the rear sight, and lining it up on the target. At this stage of the instruction that's all your wife needs to know.

Select a target for the first sessions which is big and near. A sizable tin can at 20 or 30 feet is ideal; it reveals a hit with a satisfying sound, and it is easy enough to hit to be encouraging. From it you can progress to smaller targets, but keep the distance within 35 or 40 feet for the spring-powered BB guns.

Urge your wife to shoot with both eyes open. She'll object, at first, saying that she sees two barrels, but will rapidly discover that she can hit the target. At first she will have to concentrate on making her right eye assume the dominant role in the sighting, but with practice she'll find that master eye doing it automatically.

In some instances you may find a right-handed person whose left eye is the master eye, in which case it is almost impossible for him to shoot from the right shoulder with both eyes open. I discovered this condition in my oldest son when he was about eight years of age, and my solution was to switch him to shooting left-handed. From that port side he can shoot with both eyes open, with the master left eye performing properly. This is the most practical solution if you encounter this problem, which is not rare.

The advantages of shooting with both eyes open are largely twofold: you can see better than with one eye, and you can judge range, speed and direction much better. The latter is most important when shooting at running or flying game.

Using a spring-powered BB rifle, the shooter can actually see the flight of the shot and correct for misses. A paper target would also reveal the errors, and we'll move to that phase a bit later. Plinking-type targets, such as a tin can, are more interesting for novices.

Under proper conditions there's another shooting game which is fun and instructional with a BB rifle but not so with a more powerful rifle. That's to shoot at floating or drifting targets on the water of a lake or stream. The little geyser of water kicked up by the BB tells where the shot went, and small piece of bark or section of a tree limb makes a good floating target.

It is dangerous, let me emphasize, to shoot at the surface of a lake or stream with more powerful rifles, since the ricochets can do damage at a great distance. It is perfectly safe with a spring-powered Daisy, however, if you have a hundred yards or so of open water before you.

Move up a step from the Daisy with rifles powered by gas (CO_2) or compressed air. Many such models are manufactured by Daisy, Benjamin, Crosman, Sheridan and Winchester, and they range from inexpensive to Olympic models selling for almost two hundred dollars. The latter are precision target rifles, capable of the highest accuracy. These rifles shoot BBs, or pellets in 177, .20 or .22 caliber. They're a bit more expensive to shoot than spring-powered BB rifles, but still less than powder guns.

With these you can teach your wife more about proper holding and trigger squeeze. Draw a picture for her to illustrate the proper alignment of the sight on the target. Then let her practice it from a steady shooting position, preferably from a solid rest, until she has the idea fully in mind. The more shooting she does, the better she'll get, and you can progress to other shooting positions as she improves. Apart from resting the gun over something solid, the prone position is the steadiest. Next is the sitting, then the kneeling, and finally—most difficult of all—the offhand stance.

With the pellet guns you can move to shooting such pests as rats, turtles, starlings and English sparrows, and even crows at short range. Make sure such gunning is legal and safe in your area.

Before your wife or children join you on hunts, instruct them in the principles of gun safety. Top, a youngster learns the safe way to go under a fence—without the gun, which she'll pull through butt first from the other side. Bottom, the proper way to hand guns across a fence.

SHOOTING INDOORS

Bullet traps are available for BBs and pellets, which allow you to shoot inside your home, and this opens up a whole new world of pleasure. Most basements, game rooms or living rooms afford enough space for a satisfactory range, and this means hours of pleasure indoors when the weather won't permit you to get outside, or when it's impossible for you to drive into the countryside to shoot.

Both Daisy and Crosman have traps for BBs and pellets, and Crosman has a "bell" target which rings when the bull's-eye is hit. Sheridan makes two models of a trap which will handle .22 rimfire as well as pellets and BBs.

Targets are important in shooting, because they lend interest and variety to the sport. Your imagination can run wild on this topic, but here are a few items which serve well: blocks of wood, potatoes, tin cans (try them filled with water), candy mints (try shooting through the hole in the middle), balloons and playing cards. With the discarded playing cards, try to shoot out the spots, and then turn a card edgewise and try to slice it in half.

One of the nice things about plinking with BBs and pellet guns is that it fits so well with other outdoor activities—camping, fishing, picnics, cookouts and the like. Weave your shooting instructional periods into such events, keeping them fun rather than drudgery, sport instead of school.

THE .22 RIMFIRE

The .22 rimfire rifle is by all odds the favorite gun in this country for plinking, target shooting and small-game hunting. It deserves the position, for it is a marvel of efficiency. The recoil is nonexistent, the report is moderate, and the accuracy is superb.

The single-shot bolt action is the safest rifle for beginners. Here, and possibly with the pellet guns, you may move to the use of peep sights rather than open sights. They are far more efficient than open sights, and inferior only to scope sights.

You'll find that your pupils wonder, at first, about the peeps. They'll feel that there is too much margin for error, but will quickly discover that the eye naturally centers the front sight in the center of the peep hole.

The scope sight is the most efficient of all, by a wide margin. Not only can the shooter see better, but as the sight (reticle inside the scope) and the target are in the same plane, it is not necessary to align rear sight, front sight and target, trying to focus the eye alternately on the three. This is difficult for young, efficient eyes, and almost impossible for those which are not so young and not so good. With the scope, when the crosshair is on the target the rifle is aligned. It is that simple.

The range of a .22 rimfire is much greater than that of a pellet rifle. This means more care in selecting a place to shoot, but opens up a greater variety of shooting possibilities. Where pellet guns are marginal to inadequate for small game such as rabbits and squirrels, the .22 rimfire is excellent.

CENTER-FIRE RIFLES

The next step up in rifles is to the center-fire, usually to a caliber suitable for deer hunting. For women and youngsters there are two superb calibers on the market now which have very moderate recoil. They are the 6mm Remington and the .243 Winchester calibers. Both are available in many rifles, and both are excellent for deer and for other big game in this size class.

Don't have your wife or child begin shooting a deer rifle until she has had considerable experience with the smaller guns. Then, when you do, make sure that she wears a jacket with padding which will protect her shoulder.

Don't tell her that there will be *no* recoil at all—instead, say that it will not be unpleasant. Let her take those first shots from an offhand or a sitting position, since recoil is less apparent than in the prone or benchrest positions. After a few rounds of firing she will learn the secret of firing a center-fire rifle: a relaxed posture, but a firm grip on the stock.

SHOTGUNS

It is usually a mistake to start your wife off on shotgunning with a .410 gauge, although this is frequently done. The thought behind the move is admirable—give her a gun that is easy to handle and pleasant to shoot. In practice

Beginners forget about recoil when swinging on a live target. This woman is shooting a double-barreled shotgun, one of the safest guns as you can always see if it's loaded.

this doesn't work out well for one reason: the .410 is also quite inefficient. It is really an expert's tool. Using it, a beginning shooter is greatly handicapped, and in the case of a wife who isn't avid to begin with this handicap may be the undoing of a hunting partnership.

The best compromise between the inefficient .410 and the potent 12 gauge is often the 20-gauge gun. This is big enough to be effective, yet does not have the healthy recoil and weight of a 12 gauge.

The single-barrel shotgun is satisfactory as a beginner's gun, but it is not ideal. Most have poor pointing qualities, and most are light in weight. The latter causes recoil to be severe in the larger gauges.

Better choices are the slide-action pump repeaters, the double barrels (either side-by-side or over-and-under), or the semiautomatics. The semiautos in the gas-operated models are particularly light in recoil and pleasant to shoot. The doubles point well, and are probably the safest shotguns to use. The pumps probably offer the most gun value for the money of any type of action.

Shotguns are designed for shooting at moving targets, and that is the way your training should be conducted. Don't have your wife or youngster shoot at a can sitting on a post, for instance, to "get them used to the shotgun."

The best training targets are clay targets. Hand traps for throwing these targets are available for less than five dollars, and one of these will free you from the necessity of going to the skeet or trap range for these first teaching sessions. After your student has a bit of experience with the shotgun, trap and skeet shooting—especially skeet—are excellent training.

HUNTING

The best way to start wife and children hunting is to just let them go with you as a spectator. This is natural—it happens that way most of the time, anyway. By going along they get the feel of the activity, without the responsibility of participating.

Some types of hunting lend themselves to family participation while others do not. It is the exceptional woman, for instance, who could handle a rugged backpacking trip into the wilderness areas, but most would have no problem on a dove hunting outing.

Hunting conditions vary tremendously throughout the country, because of the nature of the terrain, the species being hunted, and the methods of hunting. A commonsensical approach to fitting your "family" activity into these situations is all that's required. A bit of judgment will avoid placing your novices into situations which aren't suitable.

Even after your wife and children grow out of the novice class insofar as hunting is concerned, there will still be hunts you'll make without them. Don't inflict your family upon your hunting buddies at times when they're obviously not welcome.

Many couples have an annual rendezvous for the deer season. Two, three, four couples or more—they meet at the appointed location and devote a week or two to "deer hunting." Their deer "camp" may be a plush lodge on their

A limit of Canada geese brings smiles to novice and teacher.

lease in west Texas, a rough shack in the north woods of Minnesota or a collection of tents which they pitch in the mountains of the west. More and more frequently, it seems, these camps turn out to be mobile vacation vehicles—pickup campers, trailers, tent trailers and motor homes.

The wives in the group, quite frequently, are not avid hunters, but the hunt affords an opportunity for friends—often from different parts of the country—to get together. The women usually do some hunting, but stay in camp to play cards or to gossip if that's their pleasure.

Dove hunting is a gregarious sport which usually finds women and youngsters participating. In many sections of the country such a hunt is a social event as well as a hunt, a festive occasion frequently marked by a fieldside cookout either before or after the hunt.

Upland bird hunting is an ideal sport for couples. The game is often found near home, and there is a minimum of hiking and hardship. *Charley Dickey photo.*

Dove hunting is usually an excellent way to indoctrinate new shooters into the sport of wing shooting. Opportunities to shoot are many, and the coach can stand by his pupil to give instructions without interfering with the sport. A dove hunt is ideal for women and children for another reason: it is physically easy. At any time, the novices can return to the auto if they tire.

HUNTING AND OTHER HOBBIES

The wife of a good friend of mine loves to accompany him to their hunting camp, but she seldoms lifts a gun against the deer, turkey, or squirrels which abound on their place. She is an avid photographer and wildlife watcher, and will stay in a hunting blind for hours indulging her chosen pursuits.

This woman became interested in photography, I should add, from the enjoyment she got from seeing wildlife while she was hunting. She wanted to capture the sights which she had experienced on film, and soon became engrossed in a hobby entirely new to her. Now, in just a few years, she has accumulated hours of good movie footage on deer, turkey, bobcats, raccoon, opossums, squirrels and birds of many kinds.

My wife has two other hobbies, besides hunting, which she blends into our outdoor outings. She collects old bottles and jugs, and she is a flower-show judge specializing in dried arrangements.

Fathers and sons close the generation gap on a deer hunt by sharing the excitement of the chase and the satisfactions of success. This man has taught his son the importance of a steady shooting position.

In most hunting areas there are abandoned homesteads, and Mary frequently spends some of her hunting time probing around these for bottles. The outdoors, of course, is *the* place to collect material for dried flower arranging, and fall—hunting time—is the best time for this collecting.

In exposing wife or children to your hunting sports, keep in mind that they probably are not physically or mentally geared to accept or tolerate the physical discomfort which most hunters consider normal. When you take them along, therefore, make special effort to see to their comfort. Don't prolong the hunt—their exposure to it—beyond the point of their endurance.

There are many small ways to lessen the physical discomfort, or eliminate it entirely, from your hunting activities. I take along shooting stools for all the members of my family when we're dove hunting, and even folding lawn chairs on occasion. Mary and the children appreciate this, but I don't mind creature comforts, either.

A thermos jug of something to drink, cold or hot depending upon the weather, is welcome on any outdoor outing. Snacks of any kind always find favor with my boys, and they are typical of the teen set.

Make sure that you equip your beginning hunters properly from the clothing standpoint. In many instances the outfits they wear for general sports activity will be entirely adequate, but if the situation calls for something they don't have, get it. If boots are needed, insist that they have them.

Many hunting situations are cold-weather situations, and call for prolonged exposure such as few wives and children usually experience. There is cold-weather clothing available now, however, which can take the bite out of any temperature.

Jackets, coats and even underwear filled with goose down are superb items for outdoor wear, even in moderately cold weather, regardless of where you live. Modern synthetics have been developed in the past decade which are also excellent.

One company which specializes in outdoor clothing and equipment, and which has outfitted most of the polar and mountain-climbing expeditions, will send its catalog upon request. The address is: Eddie Bauer, 417 East Pine Street, Seattle, Washington 98122.

Some years ago a friend of mine built a sizable deer camp designed as a "men only" operation. After a few years his wife went with him on one trip, and soon found that she wanted to tag along all of the time. Then the wives of relatives and finally the sons-in-law and daughters-in-law were joining the party.

The camp is one huge room in which the men slept dormitory style, but the scene has changed. Now the camp has been divided into a series of compartments separated by curtains, to afford privacy for the various family groups. During the daytime the curtains are pulled back to the walls and the camp is one big room again.

I hunted there with my two sons this past winter, and found a situation illustrating—in the extreme—the enjoyment of hunting by families. In camp were my friend's wife, their son and his wife, their grandson and his wife, and their great-granddaughter. The latter, only two years old, elected not to hunt, but she did join her parents on the deer stand for a few hours one day.

This camp still has "men only" hunts, but during part of the season the wives and children are welcome. It follows that these wives don't feel like "hunting widows" with "hunting orphans." How much better it is to leave a smiling wife at the door when departing on a hunt, which is usually the situation when she has experienced the joys of hunting with you—and knows she will again.

Archery is a good sport for keeping youngsters occupied in the camp area. After they develop their skill on targets, they can join their father on bowhunts.

ARCHERY

Bowhunting has been practiced for hundreds of years, but this sport has mushroomed in popularity in the last decade or two. Shooting a bow, whether at targets or for hunting game, lends itself beautifully to our list of outdoor activities suitable for families.

Our archery equipment is a standard item on the checklist when we pack for camping, whether the camping is part of a travel trip, for hunting or fishing, or just camping for camping's sake. Shooting a bow is a fun way to spend hours right around camp, and one of the advantages is that this is a quiet pastime which doesn't disturb the tranquility of the area.

Pickup camper serves as a "tree stand" for this archer on a bowhunt.

There is little question but that bowhunters become better naturalists for having begun the sport. The nature of the activity requires that they attempt to blend unobtrusively with the setting, and in doing so they see and hear birds and animals which escape most gun hunters.

If you aren't an archer, consider becoming one. This is an outdoor sport which is very simple, and which you can enjoy with your family at home or on trips.

Bows are sold by bow "weight," which is the number of pounds of force required to pull the bow the length of a standard arrow. Make sure you select a weight which is suitable. This may be a 15-pound pull for young children, and should not be more than 35–40 pounds even for you if you're a novice. The most frequent mistake of beginners is using a bow which is too difficult for untrained muscles to pull.

All archery manufacturers offer free catalogs, and some have booklets on equipment selection and archery training. Some of the larger manufacturers are: Bear Archery Company, Grayling, Michigan 49738; Ben Pearson, Inc., Pine Bluff, Arkansas 71601; Shakespeare Company, Kalamazoo, Michigan 49001; Browning Arms Company, 1706 Washington Avenue, St. Louis, Missouri 63100; and Wing Archery Company, Jacksonville, Texas 75766.

BLAZE ORANGE

One of the greatest safety aids for hunting with firearms is a new color called Blaze Orange. It is so effective at preventing "I-thought-he-was-a-deer" accidents that some states now require big-game hunters to wear this color.

Blaze Orange resembles no color or shade found in nature, and it retains its vividness as long as any daylight exists. The traditional red color fails miserably at the time of day when it is most needed, since it appears black at the low light levels of early morning and late afternoon. Those are the times when game animals are most active.

Most clothing manufacturers now have hunting garments of Blaze Orange in their line. Blaze Orange capes, which fit over any kind of clothing, are very popular, and they fold into a small package for storage when not needed. Caps of this brilliant color are now available in most sporting goods stores, and offer a great measure of protection from accidental injury.

Blaze Orange apparel has received most attention for big-game hunting, but it is fully as valuable—I think more so—for upland bird hunting. In the thick coverts where most of us hunt grouse, pheasants, woodcock and quail this kind of gear is extremely valuable.

Despite the emphasis which this book places on safety, keep in mind that hunting is one of the safest of the sports. You are in much more danger while driving to and from the hunting area than you are while afield with a gun.

SOURCES OF INFORMATION

There are a number of excellent books available on how to teach the various kinds of shooting, and on how to hunt the various kinds of game animals and birds. If you feel that you need help in a particular area, seek out the appropriate volume and use it as a guide.

The following organizations, in addition, have available free booklets and other information about shooting and shooting sports: National Shooting Sports Foundation, 1075 Post Road, Riverside, Connecticut 06878; National Rifle Association, 1600 Rhode Island Avenue, N.W., Washington, D.C. 20036; Winchester Arms Company, New Haven, Connecticut; Remington Arms Company, Bridgeport, Connecticut; and Savage Arms Company, Westfield, Massachusetts.

2 Competitive Shooting

COMPETITION IS the name of the game in the United States, whether it be in the free-enterprise business world or in sports. A great segment of our population participates in such competitive athletic sports as baseball, football, basketball, hockey and track when they are in school, and follow them avidly as spectators in later life. Many continue to be active in golf, tennis, handball, swimming and bowling.

It is not unnatural, therefore, that competitive shooting of various kinds also occupies a prominent place in the field of outdoor activities. It began in the early days of this nation, and history is sprinkled with references to shooting matches and turkey shoots where frontiersmen competed with flintlocks.

BB GUNS

Where your wife and children are concerned, odds are good that shooting competition will begin with BB-gun instruction. We are a competitive people, and not many sessions of instruction will pass before somebody says, "Bet I can hit that can and you can't."

Although shooting at targets such as tin cans is more fun for a beginner, most will soon want to move to a target which will preserve the record of their accuracy. The most common such targets have the circular bull's-eye, with concentric scoring rings surrounding it, but there are many other kinds available which offer variation. Some have silhouette targets of crows, squirrels or woodchucks, and Daisy has one paper target which has thirty-nine separate "pop-out" bulls. If you hit the bull's-eye on these, it pops out of the target.

Daisy, the oldest and by far the largest firm in the field of BB shooting, is located at Rogers, Arkansas 72756. The company made and sold more than fifty-four million BBs *a day* in 1968, convincing evidence that a lot of people enjoy plinking with this gun.

Competitive shooting for young people usually begins with BB rifles. Although plinking at tin cans is good practice, shooting at paper targets allows beginners to keep a record of their accuracy.

The armed forces are using BB guns extensively in training combat troops. The final week of training at Fort Polk, Louisiana for troops headed for Vietnam was with BBs, in a "quick-kill" program designed to teach the recruits to shoot instinctively.

The advantages of using BB guns in such a program are many. Two of the most important are that their use reduces the cost of the training tremendously, from an ammunition standpoint, and it sharply reduces the acreage needed for such a training program. With BBs, the quick-kill ranges can be side by side, whereas a separation of hundreds of yards would be necessary if live ammunition were being used.

Hundreds of thousands of boys, who enjoyed this BB-shooting phase of training, are returning to civilian life to find that Daisy has available an adaptation of the program for civilians. It's called "Quick Skill," and the kit contains a BB rifle, a supply of BB shot, protective shooting glasses, aluminum disc targets and instructions.

Most people can quickly learn to hit the discs when they're tossed into the air, and this becomes a sport in itself. The shooting glasses are for protection from BBs which might ricochet from the targets.

INDOOR SHOOTING

The absence of report of the spring-powered Daisys makes them ideal for indoor shooting. A suitable backstop for the BBs can be made by stuffing a cardboard box full of newspapers. Daisy also has two kinds of indoor backstops on the market—their Targetex Portable Target, and the Official Daisy BB Range.

Being able to shoot indoors opens up a whole new field of possibilities. No longer are shooters restricted to daylight hours, nor to days when the weather is good.

FORMAL COMPETITION

In 1966 Daisy and the U.S. Jaycee began a shooting education program. That year it taught gun safety and the fun of shooting to some 300,000 youngsters from seven to fourteen years of age. The number has grown each year since then.

Each participating local Jaycee chapter conducts its own program, which in the final stages includes competition to determine the five best BB shooters taking the course. Those five become the team representing that chapter, and successive team competition results in a state winner being determined. Those winning state teams compete each summer in the Annual International BB Gun Championship, which is one of the most wholesome gatherings of American youth it has ever been my pleasure to observe.

Check with your local Jaycee chapter to see if they are participating in the program. If not, urge them to do so, for it is difficult to conceive of a more worthwhile project. Odds are good that your youngster, boy or girl, would enjoy and benefit from this fine program.

Competition with the spring-powered BB guns is at a range of 15 feet, and the air rifle most used is the Daisy Model 99. It is the official gun for the Jaycee International Championship, and is approved for Boy Scout, 4-H and NRA matches.

The NRA is the National Rifle Association, an organization which is the hub of rifle and pistol shooting competition in this country. It is an excellent organization with Junior and Senior memberships of more than one million. It publishes a monthly magazine called *The American Rifleman,* and has a wide range of competitive shooting programs under its sponsorship.

There are hundreds of rifle and pistol clubs in the country which are affiliated with the NRA, and odds are good there is one near you. If you're interested in joining such an organization, which provides fellowship, helpful guidance from experienced shooters, and usually a shooting range, inquire about such a club at your local sporting goods store. If need be, you can get such information concerning nearby clubs directly from the NRA at 1600 Rhode Island Avenue, Washington, D.C.

The NRA also has programs of marksmanship achievement in which members can participate via the mails. Members fire their qualifying targets anywhere, and send their scores to Washington. I first began competitive shooting in this fashion more than three decades ago, and still recall the great pleasure I got from the medals which are the rewards for achieving successive levels of skill.

The NRA also has a new 333 Air Rifle Program, popularly called the 10-meter program. This was especially created for the more sophisticated, adult shooter, but it is equally popular with many advanced youngsters.

As the name indicates, the shooting distance in this program is 33 feet—or 10 meters. Any air or carbon-dioxide (CO_2) rifle of .22 caliber or smaller, firing pellets or spherical BB shot and weighing not more than 12 pounds, may be used.

Such a distance as this may be found in or around most homes—basement, recreation room, hallway or patio, and the backstops for the shooting are no problem. With pellet guns you'll need more layers of newspaper in that cardboard box than with BB rifles, but the commercial backstops will handle either.

Air-rifle shooting, with pellet guns, is a widespread and important sport in Europe. Shooting leagues along the lines of our bowling leagues are common, with whole families often participating. The trend is moving in this direction, and more and more such operations will be found in the U.S. in the coming years.

One thing should be emphasized. The best air rifles are not toys, but precision instruments capable of superb accuracy. They have rifled barrels and the best adjustable peep sights, and the top lines sell for almost $200. They are inherently more accurate than the best match .22 rimfire rifles available.

To illustrate what is happening in the field, consider that air-rifle shooting will be an official part of the program at the 1972 World Olympics. The same will be true at the World Shooting Games, to be held in Arizona in 1971.

Another plus in favor of air-rifle shooting is that neither air rifles nor pistols are included in the 1968 federal firearms laws. That being the case, a dealer does not have to have a federal firearms license to sell them, and youngsters below the age of eighteen can buy them.

PISTOLS

What I've said for air rifles also applies to air pistols, but on a lesser scale. There are fewer competitive programs available for them, but more are on the way. The gas-powered (CO_2) pistols are great fun for plinking, and for teaching wife or youngsters the rudiments of pistol shooting.

Some hunting *is* done with pistols, but it is unusual. For that reason I've reserved comments on handguns for this chapter.

Handling a pistol requires special safety precautions, since the short barrel can inadvertently be pointed toward someone very easily. Make sure that your "students" rigidly adhere to all rules of gun safety when handling these short-barreled arms. If you keep a pistol in your home for protection, which seems to be more and more necessary as the crime rate rises, it is especially important that each member of your family knows how to treat it. For your wife, and those children at a sufficiently responsible age, this means knowing how to handle it.

Air pistols such as the Daisy CO_2 Model 200 have become popular as aids for dog trainers. A stinging, but harmless, shot from one of these will usually restore a dog's respectful attention when it is out of arm's reach of the trainer.

Big-game hunters in the West frequently carry the Model 200 along for potting grouse for the table. It's ideal for this short-range shooting because there is no report to spook deer or elk from the area.

It is only a short step from air pistols to the 22-rimfire handguns, and most wives and youngsters really enjoy shooting these. Recoil is negligible, and accuracy of the better revolvers and semiautomatics is excellent.

Handgun competition is done with the 22 rimfire, and the .38- and .45-caliber center-fires. Most ladies prefer to limit their shooting to the rimfire, but there are some excellent female shooters with all three.

Unless you are a competition pistol enthusiast, it is unlikely that your wife will get the bug for this phase of the shooting game. If you own a handgun, odds are good that she will enjoy sharing your plinking and practice sessions.

In a home where a handgun is kept, the housewife should know how to use it. Even if she cares nothing about shooting it for sport, she should be familiar with the mechanics of unloading it, loading it and shooting it.

SMALL BORE

Small-bore competition is the name applied to matches in which .22 rimfire rifles are used, and there are probably more of these taking place throughout the nation than any other kind. This .22 rimfire is usually the first real gun for most youngsters, once they have passed the Daisy stage, since the very efficient pellet rifles are just now becoming important in the overall picture.

Mild report and almost no recoil—these are two big advantages of this caliber. It is, in addition, very accurate and relatively inexpensive.

Small-bore shooting is the backbone of most rifle and pistol clubs, and most towns of any size have such a club. Most of them have weekly competition between the members, and frequent shoots in competition with neigh-

Young shooters practice two positions used in competition—prone and sitting.

boring clubs. Once or twice a year most of them have larger meets, with shooters gathering from several states for the shoulder-to-shoulder firing.

Clubs also compete with other units in "mail" shoots. Each member fires on his own range, then the scores are exchanged to determine winners.

In all of these shoots, competition is divided into classes. The youngsters compete against others of their age group; ladies against ladies; and men against men. This is standard practice for most shooting competition.

BIG BORE

Here we're talking about center-fire rifle shooting, which is the companion competition to small bore in most clubs. The mechanics of this phase are the same as for the .22 rimfire, except that shooting is often done at longer distances.

Noise and recoil are substantially greater in big-bore shooting, of course, and both are more noticeable than when the same calibers are used for hunting. One of the reasons for this is that target competition requires more shooting, and another is that the excitement of the hunt is absent.

Take your time about introducing your wife or youngsters into this phase of competition. Stay with the rimfire until you know they're ready for center fire.

BENCHREST

This is a specialized form of rifle shooting in which the rifle is fired from a shooting table called a benchrest. Here most of the problems of holding the rifle are eliminated, with the premium being placed on the shooter's ability to get the shot away in the same identical way each time, and on the accuracy of the rifle itself.

In this field of competition there is endless experimenting with barrels, stocks, methods of bedding the action and barrel into the stock, sights, triggers and

Benchrest is needed for sighting-in a rifle before a match. Rests are also used in formal competition in which rifles are tuned to pinpoint accuracy.

cartridges. The goal is to find a rifle and cartridge combination which will put all the bullets through the same bullet hole. It almost takes that kind of performance to win national matches in this field now.

TRAP AND SKEET

Trapshooting is the most popular competitive shotgun sport in this country. It involves shooting at clay targets thrown at unexpected angles from a low traphouse directly in front of the shooter.

The first "trapshooting" began in England in the eighteenth century, and the targets released from the traps were live birds. This carried over into this country, but as time passed shotgun enthusiasts also used wooden blocks, tin cans and bottles as targets. The glass ball, however, was the first substantial replacement for live birds in trapshooting.

The spherical glass ball, however, does not simulate the flight of a bird very closely, and some years later a Cincinnati shooter invented the clay target. This clay "pigeon," essentially the same as we know it today, was the substitute bird which sent trapshooting off and running.

Most trap and skeet ranges have a clubhouse where women can watch the shooting, play cards or watch television.

In 1890 the Interstate Trapshooting Association was formed. As the regulating body of the sport, it held championship shoots beginning in 1900, and these have continued to this day. In 1923 this organization became known as the Amateur Trapshooting Association (ATA), and the following year a permanent home was built at Vandalia, Ohio.

Vandalia, each August, is the scene of one of the greatest shooting spectacles of all time. It is the Grand American Trapshoot, and in recent years more than 3,000 shooters have stood shoulder-to-shoulder to compete in the feature event.

The "Grand" lasts for a full week, and it is seven days of fun for the many families which make this an annual affair. A high percentage of wives and children accompany the men, and many of them join in the competition.

This event has all the earmarks of a gigantic camp-out, and it is that. Hundreds of the contestants bring tents, campers and trailers, filling all available space on the "Grand" grounds and spreading out into surrounding commercial campsites. Many of these families have been attending for years, and when they gather at Vandalia from throughout the nation it resembles an economy-sized family reunion.

Just what is this trapshooting, which has lasted so long and which attracts so many shooters?

In trapshooting there are five shooting positions, numbered consecutively from 1 to 5, left to right facing the traphouse. Five targets are shot at from each post, then each of the five shooters on the squad moves to the next station to repeat the process. The twenty-five shots, five from each station, constitute a "round."

The clay targets are thrown from an oscillating trap so that the shooter does not know the path a specific target will take. It may vary as much as 44 degrees from one extreme to the other, but the angle of rise is constant.

There are three events in trapshooting: singles, handicap and doubles. In singles all shooters fire from a position 16 yards behind the traphouse. In handicap, firing is done from positions varying from 18 to 27 yards behind the house, depending upon the proven skill of the shooter. In doubles, all shoot from the 16-yard position, and at two targets which are released simultaneously. One is an extreme left-hand angle; the other an extreme right-hand angle.

Installation of a trap range requires a minimum amount of room and a minimum of expense. As a consequence, there are ranges scattered throughout the nation.

Trapshooting is a great sport for a family, with most gun clubs welcoming wives and youngsters. Members of these clubs are always willing to help with the instruction of novice shooters. Most ranges are open on weekends, when youngsters are out of school.

In a relatively short time your wife and youngsters can acquire the skill to hit any of the singles trap targets. The key to good scores is being able to hit them all—or most of them—and the key to this is concentration.

If the shooter lets his mind wander to such things as taxes or how things are going back at the office, he is apt to miss. Since youngsters aren't concerned with these things, they rapidly acquire the ability to shoot excellent scores. When they call for the target, they're thinking about shooting that target and about nothing else.

Wives, to a lesser but still significant extent, are able to do the same thing, so this is a mild warning to husbands that their spouse and offspring may quickly be able to compete with them in trapshooting.

When teaching trapshooting, one technique is very useful. That is to set the trap to throw the same angle target each time. Let your pupil shoot it until he or she has confidence in handling that particular angle, then reset the trap to another one.

With proper instruction and sufficient practice, many women become skilled trap and skeet shooters, their enthusiasm for the sport growing with their increased proficiency.

Trap and skeet shooters should wear ear protectors when on the range.

This can't be done, of course, when shooting a regular round, but there are many times when a range will be free. You can also make arrangements, at most clubs, to use the range for such training when the club is not officially open.

Skeet is a purely American version of clay target shooting. It originated in Massachusetts in the 1920s, when a group of upland game hunters tried to devise a sport which would be better practice for game birds than is trap-shooting.

The idea was introduced to the public in 1926, when a national contest was held to find a name for the game. Mrs. Gertrude Hurlbutt, of Dayton, Montana, won it with her suggestion of "skeet," which is an old Scandinavian form of the word "shoot."

Skeet differs from trap in a number of ways. There are two traphouses instead of one. Targets from the "high house" emerge 10 feet above ground level on an essentially level flight. Those from the "low house" emerge 3½ feet above ground level with a rising flight.

There are eight shooting positions in skeet. Seven of them are in a semicircle from one traphouse to the other, and number 8 station is midway between the houses. Each shooter fires at one high-house and one low-house target from each position, and at doubles from stations 1, 2, 6 and 7. The one extra shell left in his box of twenty-five is used as an optional, a second chance at the first target he misses. If he doesn't miss, he uses it on any target of his choice.

In both trap and skeet, shooters are grouped in classes according to proven ability, so that in competition they shoot against others of like skill. There is no handicap in skeet as in trap, but there are events with four different-gauge shotguns—12 gauge, 20 gauge, 28 gauge and .410 gauge.

Using the smaller gauges in skeet is practical, although scores decrease with the size of the shell, because skeet targets are broken at short range. In trap-shooting all shots are at relatively long range, so only with a 12 gauge can a shooter compete effectively.

This does not mean, of course, that you can't have a lot of fun shooting trap with a 20 gauge, for instance. I consider this the ideal gauge as a starting gun for most wives and youngsters, and in practice—when nobody else is shooting—you can move your pupil up close behind the traphouse.

Installing a skeet range is more involved and more expensive than installing a trap range. It requires more room, since the direction of fire covers a wider arc, and there are two traphouses and two traps. For these reasons, there are not as many skeet ranges as there are trap fields, but they are still widespread enough that most sizable towns have them.

Skeet is the game chosen by the air force as a training aid for gunners, since it develops the principles of swing and lead, so most air bases have skeet ranges. Some of these are open to the public at certain times.

Members of skeet and trap clubs are ultra-safety conscious, therefore these ranges are excellent places for your wife or children to observe good safety practices in action. Any tendency on their part to be lax with their gun handling will be quickly observed—and quickly corrected—by members and range officers.

Most skeet and trap ranges have clubhouses which overlook the range, and where wives can gather to play cards, watch television or talk while their husbands are shooting. Even if your wife doesn't shoot, she can enjoy a social afternoon at the gun club while you're on the line. Many of them do.

GUNS FOR COMPETITIVE SHOOTING

Guns which are suitable for the average man have stocks which are too long for most wives and youngsters. With such a tool, they can never develop as they should. A competent gunsmith can correct this by properly cutting off the required amount.

There are "Junior" models of some guns which are available, and others may be ordered with any stock length desired. Custom stock builders can also build just what the shooter wants.

As mentioned earlier, the Daisy Model 99 is the choice of most in the spring-powered matches, notably the Jaycee-Daisy program. It has a lever-cocking action, adjustable peep sights, a sling, and sells for less than $20.

Moving to the pellet rifles powered by CO_2 cylinders, we find these suitable for target competition: Crosman Model 160, single-shot, .22-caliber pellet rifle, about $44 with sling; Hammerli Match Rifle Model 472, at about $125. There are many other CO_2 rifles on the market which are great fun to shoot, but without the aperture sights necessary for serious competition.

In the pneumatic air-powered field, where the pellet is propelled by compressed air which is built up by a series of "pumps," the Sheridan Air Gun with Williams Sheridan receiver sight does a good job in the target field. With half a dozen pumps, it will also dispatch close-range pests.

Benjamin and Crosman also manufacture pneumatic air rifles.

The top of the line in the "air" field, where accuracy is concerned, are those air-powered rifles which are cocked with a single stroke of a lever, or a single breaking down of the barrel. Good choices for competitive shooting include: Winchester's Models 427 ($39.95), 435 ($54.95), 450 ($84.95) and 333 ($169.95); Daisy's Model 440 (about $39.95), Model 460 ($49.95), and Model 150 ($169.95); Hy-Score Model 809 Target Rifle ($64.95), and Model 810 Olympic International Rifle ($139.95); and the Savage Anschutz Model 250 ($169.95).

There are less expensive air rifles of this sort, of course. Both Daisy and Winchester, for instance, have models at about $16.00.

Rifles for .22-rimfire competition are manufactured by almost all of the gun companies. Here are some good choices in widely varying price ranges: Mossberg M320B single shot, about $32.90; Mossberg 144LS Target Rifle, $59.95; Remington Model 540X Match Target Rifle, about $100; Remington 40XB Rim Fire, about $200; Winchester Model 52, about $160; Savage Anschutz target rifle from $157 to $355; Mossberg 320B, a single-shot Boy Scout Target Rifle with peep sight, about $27.

Both Remington and Winchester have international free rifles available, the Winchester Model 52 in .22 rimfire, and the Remington in both rimfire and center-fire.

By the time you have progressed to this point, you'll need no help in choosing a rifle for center-fire competition or benchrest competition.

A shotgun for competitive trapshooting should be a 12 gauge, either full or modified choke, with a barrel length of from 28 to 32 inches. Trap and skeet guns should have a ventilated rib barrel, which dissipates the heat from continuous firing, eliminating the mirage which can affect the sight picture.

Any shotgun fitting those specifications can be effective in competition, but most trapshooters also use a gun with a "trap" stock. Such a stock is straighter than one for field use, and causes the gun to shoot a bit higher than the eye is looking. This provides a built-in lead for the rising trap targets.

At one time all trapshooting was done with full-choke barrels. In the past decade, however, new developments in shotshells have effectively "tightened" patterns, and many shooters now use a modified choke on 16-yard targets. For handicaps, and for the second target in doubles, they use full choke.

Shotguns which are seen along the trap line in numbers include the Browning Over-and-Under, Kreighoff O & U, Winchester 101 O & U, Winchester Model 12 pump (now discontinued, except for limited production of an $800 grade), Remington Model 870 pump, Remington Model 1100 semiautomatic, Ithaca

Single Barrel Trap Gun, and Winchester Model 1200 pump gun. The over-and-under doubles are preferred for doubles shooting because of their reliability, but the Remington Model 1100 semiautomatic has been gaining in this event.

For skeet shooting, any shotgun except a single shot can be used. In competition, it should have an open boring since the ranges are short. It can be any gauge, since there are events for all. (A 16 gauge could be used in the 12-gauge event, although the shooter would be at a slight disadvantage.)

Serious skeet shooters who participate in all of the gauge events prefer to have all of their guns alike. Until 1969, the only models available in 12, 20, 28 and .410 gauge were the Browning Superposed, the Winchester 101, the Kreighoff O & U, and the Remington Model 48 semiautomatic. Then Remington came out with 28 and .410 versions of the very popular Model 1100 semiautomatic, and for the Model 870 pump. Both were already available in the 12 and 20 gauges.

The Model 1100 now dominates skeet shoots as no other shotgun ever has. It is a gas-operated semiautomatic which has very light recoil, and this is important to competition shooters who may have to fire hundreds of shells in a day. For this same reason—this lack of punishing recoil—it is a fine choice for lightly built ladies or youngsters.

Barrel length on skeet guns should be 26 inches in the case of pumps or semiautos, and either 26 inches or 28 inches in the case of over-and-unders.

Although not as popular on trap and skeet fields, excellent trap and skeet guns are available from Ithaca, Stoeger, Savage and High Standard.

In all competitive shooting there are accessories which increase effectiveness, safety or comfort. In rifle shooting a sling is a must. When you are serious about your target shooting, a rifleman's coat with padded elbows is an advantage. It is tight fitting and bulky, and reduces your "wiggle" to a minimum. Gloves and mitts are useful.

For all competitive shooting with rifle or shotgun, equip your wife and youngsters with protection for ears and eyes. Long exposure to gunfire can irreparably damage the hearing, and there is always the possibility of a malfunction which could damage or destroy the eyesight.

Protection is simple. Best for the ears are the earmuffs similar to those worn by airport personnel during jet engine start-ups. The Noisefoe Mark II, made by Mine Safety Appliances Company, is excellent. Other good ones are the American Optical Company AO Hearing Protectors, which come with either a top band or a back band; and the Willson Sound Barriers. Many shooters use the Lee Sonic Ear-Valv.

Shooting glasses with impact-resistant lenses are the best answer to eye protection while shooting. They are available in clear glass, green, gray and yellow, and can be ground to the wearer's prescription if necessary. Excellent ones are the Bausch & Lomb Ray-Bans, the Mitchell Shooting Glasses, and the Bushnell Shooting Glasses. They range in price from about $15 to $45 in the non-prescription glass.

If you do very much shooting with shotguns or center-fire rifles, you should consider reloading your own shells and cartridges. This is an easy process for anyone who will follow simple directions, and results in a substantial financial savings. This is particularly true when several members of the family shoot.

Many competitive big-bore shooters also reload in the interest of better accuracy. With care, reloads can be tailored for a particular rifle to get better groups than with factory ammo.

Several good reloading manuals are on the market. Two good handbooks for rifle cartridges are the Speer Manual, from Speer, Lewiston, Idaho; and the Hornady Handbook, from the Hornady Manufacturing Company, Grand Island, Nebraska 68801.

There are certain organizations which govern and/or promote competitive shooting of various kinds, and all are eager to help beginning shooters with information and instruction. Feel free to contact any of these for guidance:

ALL SHOOTING SPORTS—National Shooting Sports Foundation, 1075 Post Road, Riverside, Connecticut 06878;

SMALLBORE, BIG BORE AND PISTOL—National Rifle Association, 1600 Rhode Island Avenue N.W., Washington, D.C. 20036 (Membership in the NRA includes a subscription to its monthly magazine, *The American Rifleman*);

TRAPSHOOTING—Amateur Trapshooting Association, Vandalia, Ohio (official publication is *Trap & Field*, 1100 Waterway Blvd., Indianapolis, Indiana 46202—$7.00 for 10 issues annually);

SKEET SHOOTING—National Skeet Shooting Association, 212 Linwood Building, Dallas, Texas 75235 (official publication is *Skeet Shooting Review*, same address, $6.00 annually);

MUZZLE LOADING COMPETITION—National Muzzle Loading Rifle Association, P. O. Box 15, Friendship, Indiana 47021 ($6.00 annual membership includes official publication *Muzzle Blasts*);

PISTOL SHOOTING—U.S. Revolver Association, 59 Alvin Street, Springfield, Massachusetts (Official publication is *The Handgunner*—$3.50 per year);

AIR RIFLE SHOOTING—NRA (above); Daisy Company, Rogers, Arkansas; U.S. Jaycees, Box 7, Tulsa, Oklahoma 74102;

CLAY TARGET COMPETITION—Winchester Arms Company, New Haven, Connecticut 06504.

3 Fishing

FISHING IS the outdoor sport which immediately comes to mind when the subject of family participation in the outdoors is mentioned. This is as it should be, for there are few activities which lend themselves more to such participation than does this one, but there are pitfalls to avoid. Using the correct approach, the angler-sportsman can insure that he and his family will have many days and weeks of pleasure together on lakes and streams, but with the wrong approach he can insure that his wife and youngsters will always have something else to do when he suggests another fishing trip.

The essential thing to keep in mind, when you are initiating your wife or youngsters into this sport, is that you must plan fishing trips specifically for them. If you expect to take them along on one of your regular outings, conducting the trip as if you were alone, then you are doomed to disappointment. There are many reasons for this.

First is that the interest span of your family is very short, when it comes to fishing, compared to your own. You may enjoy hour after hour of casting or cane poling or trolling, but probably your wife and youngsters will not. The first rule of initiating your family into the sport, then, should be to keep it short.

Next you must realize that your family's tolerance of discomfort is much less than yours where fishing is concerned. Although the average fisherman will spend hours on a lake in bitter cold weather, sitting on a hard, uncomfortable boat seat, or stumbling over rocks and boulders in a stream, it is unreasonable to expect novices such as beginning wives and children to do so. You must plan for their comfort on these outings to a much greater degree than you would ever consider doing for yourself.

The timing of that first trip is important. Don't choose a day that is bitter cold or blazing hot or threatening rain. Make your choice, in other words, so that your chances of having a comfortable, enjoyable outing are greatest.

The kind of fishing you choose depends upon several things. Your location is one, of course, since you will usually have to work with the species at hand. Cane pole or casting? That will depend upon your family, too.

Most of the time, where children are concerned, the cane pole is best, and the bluegill is a perfect fish because it usually provides enough action to keep the interest high. With wives, on the other hand, learning the mechanics of casting in your backyard may be the springboard to whet her appetite for the real thing.

CANE POLE FISHING

Cane poles come in a wide assortment of sizes and quality. Even the best is inexpensive, so buy that. It will be treated to make it stronger and more resistant to water damage, and it will be light in weight. The latter is important.

Most young arms will quickly tire from the task of handling a long, heavy, unwieldy pole, so choose one about 8 feet in length. Tie to it a length of 10-pound-test monofilament about the same length as the pole. The best hook to use is a long-shanked size 8 or 10 made from soft wire.

The long shank is a big advantage when removing the hook from a bluegill's mouth. The soft wire permits the hook to straighten out rather than break when it hangs on an underwater obstruction, which it will frequently do in most bluegill habitat.

Use a small, brightly colored float, for nothing so intrigues beginning fishermen as the dimple of the "cork" when a fish nibbles, and its disappearance when a bluegill really bites. To be perfectly truthful about it, I get much more pleasure fishing this way than by fishing a "tight line," even when the latter would take more fish.

Fishing a tight line is simply fishing without a float. An experienced angler can feel the bite, and can experiment with depth more easily than with a float.

The float, on the other hand, adds a tremendous amount of visual pleasure. It also serves to keep the bait at a given depth, preferably at the depth where most of the fish are.

Earthworms are the universal bait for bluegills and other sunfish of this type. They are readily available almost anywhere, and are effective.

Nicer to handle than worms are the gray crickets which are raised extensively for fish bait. In most situations they are even better than are worms.

Worms can be kept in that traditional "can of dirt," but there are better and cleaner ways. It will appeal to your novices if you use one of the prepared worm bedding mixtures, which offer both food and home. There are several on the market, most similar to the "Mr. Worm" product marketed by Weber Tackle Company. These keep the worms in good condition, much more attractive for handling by your novices.

Crickets are kept in wire containers of several designs. The most popular are the cylinder with a funnel and stopper in one end, and the box type. The cylinder is a bit easier to carry, but takes a little more effort to use since

Cane pole is the ideal rod for the beginning angler. Best length is about 8 feet, with the same length of 10-pound-test monofilament line attached to the end.

two hands are required. If the fishing is hot and heavy, which it can easily be in bluegill fishing, the box type is the one I prefer. It has a big opening in the middle through which you can reach a hand to grab a cricket.

How you fish for bluegills depends largely upon the type of water you're fishing and the time of year. During the spring the fish move into the shallows to spawn, so shallow fishing is the rule. At other times of the year, particularly in the deeper reservoirs, bluegills can be quite deep.

Vary the depth you fish, by adjusting the float, until you locate fish. Pinch onto your line one or two split shot sinkers about 4 to 6 inches above the hook, and the weight will take your bait directly down to the depth you set. Using the weight is an advantage in controlling the line when swinging it into a fishing spot, and helps a great deal in getting the bait right where you want it when fishing around brush.

It is much easier to indoctrinate your beginners into cane pole fishing from the bank or from a pier if that is practical. Under these circumstances you don't have the added burden of handling a boat, caring for your charges where boating etiquette and manners are concerned, and fighting any wind which happens to be blowing.

There are few lakes and streams which harbor bluegills, fortunately, where some cannot be caught along the shore most of the time. Perhaps those in very shallow water won't run as large as those out farther, but to a beginning youngster just any fish is a trophy. Farm ponds are plentiful in most areas, and these are usually good spots to begin your fishing instruction.

Bluegills aren't the only fish to be caught with cane poles, of course. Even when fishing for bluegills, you are quite likely to hook a bass, crappie or catfish—if these species are in the water you're fishing.

CASTING

Spincasting is the easiest form of casting, and as such is the best bet for your children if they are beginning quite young. This spincast reel—often called the closed-face spinning reel—is a purely American invention, and one which caused a revolution in the fishing tackle field.

The spincast reel is controlled by a pushbutton, and the act of casting is a simple matter of holding the button down firmly with the thumb, and releasing it at the proper time during the cast. There are many models of spincast reels on the market. Stay with the well-known brand names, avoiding the very cheapest models, and you will find them satisfactory for your beginners.

One thing about spincast reels which you should look for is the position of the control button. On some it is in such a high position, so far from the rod handle, that it is difficult for small hands to handle. Select one which is suitable.

Rod length should be 5 to 6 feet, and any of the popular brands have good models. Again, select equipment which is light in weight.

The open-face spinning reel is more efficient than is the spincast reel, but is more difficult to use. You must be the judge as to whether to start your wife, or older children, on this form of fishing.

The same is true of bait-casting tackle. The casting reel has a revolving spool which requires considerable skill to use. In many respects it is superior to either the spincast or the spinning outfit, but it is not usually the best equipment for the beginner.

Fly casting is not as difficult as many believe it to be. There are aspects to the art which are beyond most anglers, and certainly beyond beginners, but most fishing does not require them.

There are many good manuals detailing the mechanics of all kinds of casting. Many of the tackle catalogs of major manufacturers include such instructions, and some of them offer separate booklets. Knowing how to cast, and knowing how to teach someone else to cast, are not the same things. Even the veteran outdoorsman, if he is not a casting instructor, could profit from these instruction booklets prior to instructing his family in the techniques.

Easiest reel for children to use is the spincast type, which is mounted on top of the rod and controlled by a pushbutton. For small hands select one with the control button close to the rod handle.

Author's wife, who is an advanced angler, lands a seatrout on bait-casting tackle. The bait-casting reel is the most difficult to use and is not recommended for beginners.

Joan Salvata conducts a casting clinic for youngsters sponsored by the Garcia Company.

Regardless of the kind of casting you're teaching, one thing applies. Do it unimpeded by actual fishing conditions. The easiest place to begin is on the back lawn, using a practice plug on the line rather than a lure. In this environment the youngster or wife is not bothered by hooks, fish or trees. The initial idea is to teach them how to cast the lure a fair distance, and only after that is accomplished should you concentrate on accuracy. When you do get to that accuracy stage, however, remember that old bicycle tires scattered across the lawn make excellent targets.

Let your pupil stand when he or she is beginning the casting practice, but later on move to a sitting position. It is from the latter that most actual fishing will be done.

The species of fish you seek once your beginners are to that stage will depend on what you usually fish for. You're grooming them to enjoy *your* sport, whether it be for trout, pike, walleye, catfish, bass or any other species.

Regardless of what kind of fishing you're asking your family members to do, keep one rule in mind. Just check to see if *you* could fish with the equipment you give them to use.

42

TROLLING

Trolling affords an opportunity for novices to fish even if they know nothing about casting or techniques. Anyone who can hold a rod can catch fish by this method.

There are fine points to this kind of fishing which are necessary for success, but you can supply them. You determine the amount of line to let out and the speed of the boat, and there are many occasions when it is just as effective to leave the trolling rods in rod holders until the strike occurs. Perhaps this kind of angling won't appeal to you, but it may be just right for your family.

Most offshore charter-boat fishing is done by trolling, and this can be a good outing for your brood. There is room on such boats for youngsters to move around freely, something which all of them like.

Until you know whether or not any of them are susceptible to seasickness, make sure your offshore trips are taken only during relatively calm weather. Various anti-motion sickness pills, such as Dramamine or Mazarine, are very helpful in many instances.

Some states do not permit trolling where a motor is used, so check the regulations where you fish.

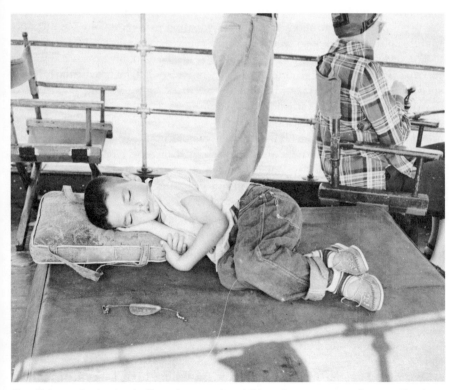

On offshore charter boats there is room for children to move around—or go to sleep.

Drifting is a form of trolling which is practiced in some areas. The usual method is to drift across a portion of a lake with the wind, then motor back to the windward side and repeat the process. When you get a strike or catch a fish, work that particular area thoroughly since you may have found a school.

Many anglers drift-fish for catfish with a variety of baits, and for bass, crappie and white bass using live minnows, but there is another technique which is less well known. That is to drift fish for bass with plastic worms, letting the lifelike lures bounce along the bottom.

CLOTHING

Dress them for the occasion. Much fishing is done in the hot sunshine of summer, and I have been witness to some very unfortunate and unhappy scenes because of that. During a period when I owned a fishing resort, I frequently had guests who took youngsters or wives out without proper protection from the sun.

Even people who have led a rather active outdoor life up until then are not usually tanned sufficiently to cope with sunshine bounced off the water for hours. Sunburn is the inevitable result, often accompanied by a ruined vacation.

Consider that long-sleeved shirts, long pants, a big floppy hat and sunglasses are often preferable to more fashionable vacation clothes. Avoid the ultra-hot middle hours of the day when the wife and youngsters are along.

The reverse is also true. If the weather is apt to be cold, or rainy, go equipped to cope with those conditions. Early mornings on a lake, particularly when speeding across the surface in a boat, tend to be chilly to cold regardless of the time of year or the latitude. It's no problem to take off layers of clothes as the temperature rises during the day, if you have them on.

A good rainsuit should be part of the gear of every fisherman, and should be with him in a boat, or near at hand on shore. Converse-Hodgeman manufactures a very lightweight, two-piece suit which is excellent. It is entirely waterproof, and can be rolled or folded into a very small package. For fishing use I prefer it in the bright orange color. This same manufacturer also markets a fishing shirt, a one-piece affair which completely covers the angler when he is sitting in a boat.

Footgear is more important than might seem at first consideration. In hot weather, boat shoes with nonslip soles are great. If the weather is apt to be cool to cold, particularly when there is a possibility that the feet will get wet, something more substantial than a canvas slipper is needed.

A pair of short rubber boots is my favorite for cool weather. Another good idea is to take along a pair of the lightweight rubber overboots. They fold into a small space, and are waterproof and warm when worn over your regular shoes.

Feet tend to suffer from cold more when fishing from a boat, since blood circulation is impeded by the sitting position and the inaction.

Sunglasses are almost a must for long hours afloat on a bright day. Continued exposure to such severe conditions without protection can actually damage the eyesight, not to mention the lesser irritation of possible headaches and eyestrain. Polaroid glasses are ideal for fishing, since they cut glare from the water in addition to reducing the direct light from the sun.

Sunglasses and a cap to shade the eyes are necessary when fishing on bright days.

FOOD, DRINK AND REST STOPS

One of the greatest aids in maintaining the interest of youngsters during the time between bites is a box of cookies and a bottle of pop, or the equivalent goodies which your children prefer. Don't make the mistake of thinking, "We don't need to take 'groceries' since we'll only be out an hour or two." Little tummies don't work that way.

Other portions of youngsters' anatomies often demand attention, so plan for more comfort stops than would be normal for adults.

WHILE YOU FISH

Although my wife is an ardent angler, and a good one, I don't try to insist that she accompany me on all of my fishing trips. When we visit a lake for a few days, she frequently elects to sleep late while I greet the dawn on the water.

A schedule which has worked well for us on many occasions calls for me fishing alone for the first two or three hours of daylight, returning to camp around eight o'clock to have breakfast with Mary. The rest of the morning we may devote to sightseeing, antique hunting or photography in the vicinity, or we may head back onto the lake if my early fishing seemed to indicate that we should.

If we sight-see in the morning, we usually nap and rest for a couple of hours after lunch, and then head for the lake to fish the late afternoon hours. If Mary goes back to the lake with me after breakfast, and we find the fish cooperative, we may stay with them through the noon hour until early afternoon. Then we quit for the day. If the objective of your outing is pleasure, don't punish yourself by fishing to the point of exhaustion.

Fishing goes hand in hand, inevitably, with water. And water means swimming and boating and sunbathing, all of them activities which often interest wives and children.

Most resorts are equipped to cater to the non-fishing members of the family as well as to the master angler. They frequently have dockside bathing beaches, playgrounds and various aquatic playthings for wives and youngsters.

Photography and bird watching, two hobbies which we'll explore in detail in later chapters, lend themselves beautifully to the fishing scene. Whether your family goes along with you in the boat (or wading or walking along a stream) or stays behind to wait for your return, they can enjoy these two activities.

My wife happens to be an artist, and her sketch pad is often a part of our equipment when we go afloat. She has spent hours capturing images on paper while I was trying to capture fish.

Whether the scene is fresh water or the coast, the shoreline is always a life-filled environment which contains creatures to interest young minds—no matter what their ages. Along the beach there are blue crabs and sand crabs, starfish and seaweed, driftwood and seashells. Along freshwater lakes and streams there is similar aquatic life.

The underwater scene opens up a whole new world which can keep youngsters occupied for hours. Skin "diving" need not necessarily be done in deep water. Even children who can't swim can be taught the use of a face mask and snorkle, and floating face down in the water using these simple items reveals new vistas for everyone. When your boys and girls are a bit older, and can really get into skin diving seriously, the possibilities are increased tremendously with the use of scuba gear.

Sons of a friend of mine accompany their father to his favorite fishing lake quite frequently but they don't fish. While their father is fishing they spend their time scuba diving for lost tackle. They find hundreds of lures, most of which fell victim to underwater snags rather than underwater lunker fish, and occasionally rods and reels. While looking for gear, they also get quite an education in underwater ecology.

The use of diving equipment, particularly scuba gear, should never be permitted without adequate instructions. Scuba instruction courses are given in most sizable towns, often through the Y.M.C.A.

Surf fishing is one of our favorite kinds of angling, and in the South where we live it is a casual, warm-water activity. For years our daughter and sons, when they were very young, would swim and romp and splash in the shallow surf between us and the beach. If conditions indicate it, fit your youngsters with small life jackets. Even if there is no danger of drowning, this can prevent them from taking an unpleasant tumble from a wave.

SAFETY AFLOAT

You should be careful, of course, whenever you fish, but when you take your family along you must be especially cautious. Try to anticipate situations which might be dangerous to your wife and youngsters, and plan ahead to cope with them.

The law requires that each boat contain a Coast Guard-approved life preserver for each person on board, and that can be in the form of either a jacket or a buoyant boat cushion. Both have drawbacks. The CG-approved jackets, although very effective, are frequently so bulky that they are uncom-

Author wears special fishing vest which inflates if he should slip in deep water.

fortable to *wear* for any length of time. The cushion, in case of an accident, is seldom around when it is needed.

There are other life-saving aids which I use, in addition to the CG-approved units. One is the San Souci vest made by the Stearns Manufacturing Company, St. Cloud, Minnesota 56301. This is an attractive and efficient vest, but most important is the fact that it is comfortable enough to *wear* while boating and fishing. It probably does not have the floating capacity of a CG-approved jacket, but the San Souci worn is much more valuable than a CG-approved jacket crammed under the boat seat.

This little gadget, the size of a cigarette pack, fits into pocket of fishing vest. A squeeze— and it inflates into a life preserver.

Stearns also markets a fine Inflatable Boater's Jacket which we have used with pleasure and confidence. It is waterproof and windproof, has a built-in hood, and can be inflated with just a few puffs.

There are a number of attractive, comfortable jackets and coats on the market now which get buoyancy from a foam lining. Among the manufacturers offering these are Converse-Hodgeman, Eddie Bauer and Stearns. These are nice looking and practical, only slightly more bulky than most regular jackets, and they will support the weight of a normal person in the water. They do not meet the CG standards.

There are other "floats" which come in a very small package, and which inflate from a CO_2 cartridge. Some are activated manually by squeezing them, while others inflate themselves once they're immersed in water. One of the latter is about the size and shape of a baseball. It can be thrown quite a distance to a person in trouble, and will inflate when it enters the water.

Although we have never needed to use one seriously, members of my family have carried (worn) a small inflatable called the Res-Q-Pak for years. It is about the size of a package of cigarettes, and has a clip to fasten it firmly to your clothing.

I make it a practice to keep one of these in my shirt pocket when I'm surf fishing, or when wading a trout stream. It makes a comfortable little bulge, a reminder that it could be a dear friend in case I step into a deep hole or am swept from my feet by the current.

One idea which has merit, when you are not actually wearing a life jacket, is to attach it to your belt or waist with a short length of cord. If you fall overboard, or the boat capsizes, your life jacket goes with you. This is particularly helpful when small children are along in a good-sized fishing boat. They have the freedom to move around without wearing a hot, bulky life jacket, yet they will be attached to it in the unlikely event of an accident.

On many occasions, when depending upon a boat cushion for protection, I have linked it to my belt with a cord. Again, I have never needed it, but that need could occur on any trip. One manufacturer formerly made a cushion with one strap having a snap arrangement to use for this purpose, but this item was discontinued when the Coast Guard ruled that it did not meet their approval. The curious reason given was that people might snap the cushion to the boat so that it would be unavailable in an emergency.

I would not like to depend upon a boat cushion to keep me afloat for hours in a big lake or the ocean, regardless of whether or not it is CG approved. In those big-water situations the only sensible kind of life preserver to count on is a Coast Guard-approved life jacket.

Regardless of how well the members of your family can swim, do not neglect the fundamentals of water safety. The "buddy" system is a time-honored and very practical idea. If a person is in trouble, his buddy can help him.

Don't dive into strange waters, no matter how deep or clear they seem, until you have examined them for depth and to make sure they are free of underwater obstructions. Don't overtax your swimming ability needlessly.

If your boat does capsize, there is one cardinal rule which applies in most instances. If the boat floats, which most will even when filled with water, stay with it until help arrives or until it floats to shore. It is much easier for rescuers to find an overturned boat than to find individual swimmers in the water. It is also very easy for a person clinging to an overturned craft to overestimate his ability to swim to the nearest shore, and such misjudgment has been responsible for the loss of many lives.

Instill in your family a consciousness of the safety fundamentals. When they have that knowledge, the probability of a crisis is small. If one does occur, your wife and children will know how to cope with it.

FISHHOOKS

Fishing means fishhooks, with the obvious possibility of danger. The greatest opportunity for getting a hook into a finger is when handling a flopping fish, and this is particularly true with youngsters who are excited over the catch.

Caution them about this, of course, and show them how to handle different species safely. A good method for novices is to use a fish "grab," a plier-like device which holds the fish securely. Another useful item is called a "Hook-Out," again a plier-like tool, which is especially handy for removing a hook deep inside a fish's mouth.

SHORE DINNERS

Break up your fishing trip occasionally with a streamside or lakeside meal. This can be a picnic menu which you bring with you, or a shoreline cookout.

Try cooking the fish you caught that morning for lunch, and you'll discover that they never tasted better. For the youngsters, especially, such an adventurous meal is just the kind of experience to make a fishing trip perfect.

You can do your cooking over a campfire, or can take along a small, one-burner stove. The latter, and a small frying pan, take up very little room in the boat.

Note that I said *you* can do the cooking. This fishing trip is intended to be recreation for your wife, and cooking a meal in a primitive setting may not be her idea of fun. If she does enjoy it, of course, there is no problem.

Another quick, easy and enjoyable lakeside affair is a wiener roast. Sticks for the roasting can be gathered along the shore, so no cooking equipment is required.

In some areas it may be either illegal or difficult to gather firewood for a cookout of this sort, so in this case consider taking along charcoal. Especially convenient for this sort of thing is the small package of charcoal about the size of the carton which holds a dozen eggs. Some of these contain their own "starter," and you simply light the whole package.

When you build a fire, whether it is from wood or charcoal, guard against wildfire. Our favorite locations for these cookouts are sandbars. There we usually scoop out a hole in the sand for the fire, and when finished we burn and bury all the debris.

There is one unique cooking stove called the "Safari Grill" which we have used with pleasure both at home for backyard cooking, in camp, and along the fishing stream. The only fuel it uses is newspapers, and a couple of double pages is enough to cook the average dish. (Safari Grill, Swaniebraai, Inc., Barr Bldg., Washington, D.C. 20006).

A handy item to have along on your fishing, in your boat, auto or pack, is a small can of charcoal starter fluid, or a solid-fuel fire starter such as that made by BernzOmatic, 740 Driving Park Avenue, Rochester, N.Y. 14613. This simplifies the task of fire building tremendously, especially in wet weather, and is most welcome if you've been caught in a downpour and need to warm up and dry out.

KEEP IT CLEAN

Regardless of what kind of fishing you're doing, leave the area in as good or better condition than when you arrived. Keep in mind that it is easier to take your cans and wrappers and other refuse back home for disposal than it was to take them to the lake or stream originally.

Burn and bury the leavings from your streamside operations, attempting to leave the spot looking as if nobody had stopped there. Don't throw empty cans, bottles, sandwich wrappers, lure boxes—anything except lures—into the lake or stream. Take them to the shore for proper disposal (burn-bury), or back home.

"Everybody else is doing it" . . . and, "Back here in this wilderness area it won't make any difference"—those are two of the most common excuses for littering, and neither is valid. There must come an end to everybody doing it, else this nation will be crushed by the refuse of civilization. As for the backcountry—nothing is more distasteful to most outdoorsmen than to find even a single empty can or bottle littering the primitive landscape.

BOATS FOR FISHING

The boat builders of this nation have done a magnificent job of producing an assortment of craft to fit almost any imaginable situation, and each year they evolve still more. Considering the tremendous range of fishing conditions from one coast to the other, it is obvious that many kinds of boats are required to cope with them.

Aluminum johnboat is the choice of many anglers for fishing in calm waters.

What boat is best for running the Snake River rapids in quest of steelhead and sturgeon? For poling along the bonefish flats of the Florida Keys? For the yellowtail run off San Diego? Portaging from lake to lake in the wilderness areas back and forth across the Canadian border? Bluegills in a farm pond?

Most of us who fish offshore do so from charter boats, so selection of a craft is no problem. The skippers who captain those charter boats have learned through experience the best kinds for their particular areas.

The kind of boat which is best for inshore saltwater fishing will depend upon whether you fish the relatively calm waters of the Gulf Coast inlets and bays, or the more severe conditions found along the Atlantic and Pacific coasts. Many of the outboard and stern-drive hulls now available are excellent for this kind of angling, with a suggested minimum length of 15 feet for calm areas and 17 feet for others.

When selecting a boat which will accommodate your family, keep in mind that it should afford more room and protection than might be required for a men-only operation.

Most anglers of this nation, however, are concerned with a boat for fishing the freshwater lakes and streams. Selection of the best one for the particular purpose must take into account: (1) the size and character of the fishing water; (2) if the boat will be carried cartop or on a trailer; (3) the number of people it must carry; (4) the question of portaging; and (5) how it will be powered.

Canoe can be portaged easily into backwoods lakes, or carried on a cartop rack to more accessible waters.

For small lakes and streams, where there is no need to cope with rough water, the aluminum version of the southern johnboat is one of the best. It is square at both ends, affording more usable room than does a pointed bow; it paddles easily and runs very well with even a small outboard motor; it is fairly stable; and it is light and relatively inexpensive.

These boats are available in a wide range of sizes. One of their disadvantages is that they are rather noisy, which can be minimized by using a mat of rubber or carpet on the floor.

For larger freshwater lakes and rivers, outboard or stern-drive hulls of aluminum or fiberglass are excellent. Especially good for family use are those with the cathedral or vee-bow design, since they are exceptionally stable.

No craft has been designed which is better for portaging, and for efficiency afloat once the carry is completed, than the traditional canoe. Some canvas canoes are still around, and some are made of fiberglass, but aluminum is by all odds the most popular material—and the best—for these sleek boats today. Those aluminum canoes which have been heat-treated will withstand rough use best.

Inflatable boats have a place in the scheme of things for fishermen and their families. Some of them are quite light and portable, and very stable. They usually will fit into the auto trunk or on the cartop luggage rack.

We have had a great deal of fun using an item which is and isn't a boat. It is an auto inner tube enclosed by a canvas cover and seat. The angler's legs protrude through holes in the seat down into the water, and the float can be used with or without waders.

There are several brands on the market. If you can't find one locally, write to Tucker Duck and Rubber Company, 2701 Kelley Highway, Ft. Smith, Arkansas 72901 and inquire about their Fish-N-Float.

Rapidly growing in popularity for family water fun, including fishing, is the pontoon boat or barge. They are usually 8 feet wide, which allows them to be trailered over the highways, but may be as much as 20 or 30 feet in length. Many have a protective roof over part of the boat, and a low fence which keeps youngsters from falling off.

Although the pontoon boats are not as maneuverable as other styles, they are quite satisfactory for many kinds of fishing. Trout, crappie, bluegills, yellow perch, white bass and catfish often lend themselves well to party boat fishing of this kind.

Another advantage of the more spacious and elaborate pontoon boats is that the family—or families—can cook, eat and move about freely on board. Some of them are available with marine toilets. Some, powered by sizable motors, are so designed that they can be used to pull water skiers. It is a very versatile boat.

In the past decade there has developed in the South a kind of fishing boat which is mushrooming in popularity throughout the nation. It is too heavy for cartop use, and certainly can't be portaged, but for the great majority of fishing conditions this is perhaps the most efficient craft of all.

A Louisiana bass fisherman designed the first boat of this type and built

Author operates the controls of his bass boat from convenient bow swivel seat. Boat is powered by stern-mounted outboard on way to fishing area; then electric bow motor takes over for silent maneuvering.

it of marine plywood. In the years since then the idea has been expanded and improved, and the boats are now constructed of fiberglass.

These boats are relatively long and narrow, but extremely stable. Several adults can actually stand on one gunnel without tipping the boat. The bow of the boat is rounded, and is of that vee-bow, cathedral design which scoops in air to give a smooth, dry ride. The gunnels are wide and overhang into the boat, giving a protected area beneath them for tackle.

These bass boats—they're equally at home fishing for other species—are fast, streamlined, very maneuverable and extremely rugged. Some of the better known brand names are the Terry Bass Boat, the Kingfisher, the Tidecraft, the Skeeter and the Hurricane.

These excellent fishing boats, in the smaller sizes, will operate beautifully with outboards of 5 to 10 horsepower, and even the smallest will safely handle motors up to 20 horsepower. The larger ones, with bigger motors, are very fast.

Optional accessories on these boats make them the most efficient fishing rigs to be found. My personal boat is a good example, typical of the ultimate (so far) development in this field, so let's examine it.

It is a 15-foot Terry Bass Boat (Delhi Manufacturing Company, Delhi, Louisiana 71232) which is 54 inches wide and weighs almost 300 pounds. It has two swivel seats on pedestal mounts, and is operated completely from the bow seat position.

The bow position is best for many reasons. Visibility is excellent, with no blind spot caused by a passenger up front or by the forward part of the boat. It is the best position for fishing, a particular advantage when fishing alone, and it is the best spot from which to operate an electric motor.

At my right hand, on my boat, are the electric start-throttle-gearshift controls for my outboard. At my left hand is a simple stick steering arrangement designed by Jim Dockery (Jim Stick, Reeves Marine, 3210 Lakeshore Drive, Shreveport, Louisiana), which is far better than a steering-wheel arrangement on a fairly small fishing boat.

On the bow I have mounted an electric motor called the Motor-Guide, surely one of the greatest boons to the angler to come along in years. (Motor-Guide, Herschede-Hall Clock Company, Starkville, Mississippi). When I have reached my fishing spot and turned off the outboard, I swing the electric motor down

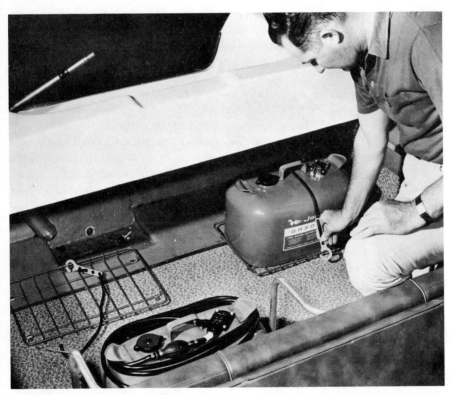

Gasoline tank should be secured in boat before leaving dock, to prevent children from kicking it over. Vinyl-covered wire holders are simple and efficient.

into the water instead of reaching for a paddle. With one foot pedal I can start and stop the Motor-Guide, and steer it in any direction.

After a few hours' practice with this remote-controlled motor, the operator doesn't even have to think. He decides the boat needs to be a bit nearer to shore . . . the boat just moves nearer to shore.

My boat is overpowered with a 55-horsepower Johnson outboard. The maximum recommended for this model is a 40 horsepower, and it will run beautifully with a 25 or 30, but I use the larger one because it is available with both an alternator and a power tilt. The alternator charges the battery even at idling speed. The power tilt is quite an advantage when operating in shallows or when beaching the boat.

My boat is also equipped with a Lowrance Depth Sounder and Fish Lo-K-Tor (Lowrance Electronics, 7809 East Admiral Place, Tulsa, Oklahoma 74115), which is an efficient aid for fishing and a pleasure to use.

These boats must be trailered, of course, and as is always true fishermen should make sure their trailer is of sufficient capacity. I use a Tee Nee Model 900, which is more than enough for boat and motor, but I know that I also use that boat in transit for a host of other equipment—gasoline, tackle boxes, ice chests, anchors and the like.

Any family vehicle, with a proper frame-mounted hitch, will easily tow a boat rig such as mine under highway conditions. As I often get into extremely rough terrain, I use a Kaiser Jeep Wagoneer. With its V-8 engine and 4-wheel-drive, I can launch and load my boat in very difficult situations where developed launching ramps are not available.

Although the occasion to use it doesn't occur frequently, I also have an electric winch mounted on the front bumper of the Wagoneer. Most families will never need one, especially if they have a 4WD vehicle, but those as dedicated to the boondocks as is my brood may find it valuable.

On a few occasions when we felt the ground was too soft or too steep even for the 4-wheel-drive, we have launched our boat by attaching the winch cable of the Wagoneer to the boat trailer. If you try this, take care that the trailer doesn't tip over, and make sure the boat is *firmly* fastened to the trailer.

My fishing rig is a rather luxurious affair, although not at all unusual on the lakes from Texas and Oklahoma to Georgia and North Carolina. From a family standpoint, one of the real advantages of an outfit like it is that wives can handle it with pushbutton ease.

Mary allows me to operate our boat if I'm along, but she has no hesitation in taking the rig out when I can't go. She can start it, steer it, tilt the motor, and "paddle" it with that electric motor with no more effort than it takes to operate a dishwasher. She knows that if a storm develops she can scoot home or to shore in minutes.

Although I tend to frown on it, I must admit that my Terry Bass Boat also operates very decently as a "ski rig." On vacation trips it frequently does double duty—fishing early and late and water skiing during the midday hours. With more power on the stern than the boat is designed for, we don't operate it at full throttle either for fishing or skiing.

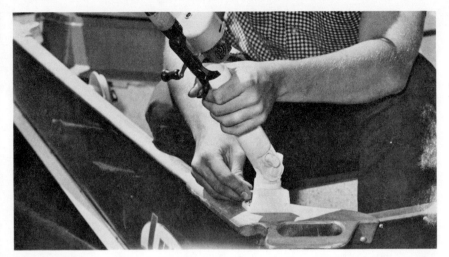

Rod holder bolts to boat gunwale, permits children who tire of fishing to rest their arms while leaving their lure in the water.

On some trips we take our "ski boat"—a 16-foot Chrysler Sport Fury powered by an 85-horsepower Chrysler outboard—and make it do double duty. Although not as efficient for most fishing as the Terry, the Sport Fury will handle bigger waters, and the "bow rider" design enables anglers to fish from the front of the boat as well as the rear cockpit.

An advantage of a bigger boat like the Fury, of course, is that there is room for five or six people. We usually fish only two in the Terry, although it will handle three easily.

All boats should have some kind of flotation material built into them. Most of the better fiberglass hulls have a form of foam flotation between the hull and the floor, as do both the Fury and the Terry. This provides rigidity, dampens sounds, and is an obvious safety factor. Canoes usually have buoyant material in the bow compartment, and also in the stern compartment except for the square-stern models.

There are so many kinds of fishing available, with such a variety of interesting surroundings, that odds are good your family will enjoy one of them. Most often, if you perform your task of indoctrination with finesse and judgment, they'll adapt to your favorite outdoor sport readily and willingly.

The simple fact is that fishing is fun, and that fishing trips provide an excuse for being in the outdoors where there are many other enjoyable activities available.

4   Camping

"SPEND OUR vacation camping? Six weeks? All five of us?" It was my wife's understandable reaction to my proposal to introduce my family to camping.

We traveled throughout much of the western part of the U.S. for a month and a half, operating out of a tent trailer, and it proved to be the most enjoyable vacation we had ever experienced. At the time daughter Barbara was thirteen, Tom was nine, and Kent eight. The situation was replete with potential for disaster, but the fact that our trip was a wonderful one only proves that camping can be fun—even for novices.

I really didn't undertake the junket lightly, having devoted hours of research and planning to it before I sprang the idea on my family. Between that time and the day we rolled from our driveway heading west, all of us learned a lot about what lay ahead.

WHY CAMP?

It's a good question, considering that more than thirty million people indulge in the activity each year, and there is not one simple answer.

Necessity was the reason for my first camping outings, all of which were associated with hunting and fishing trips. There just were no accommodations in the hunting and fishing areas we wanted to work, which meant that living in the field was a necessity if we were to enjoy those areas.

That condition still exists, in many places, and I hope the situation never changes. There should always remain remote portions of the outdoors which are beyond the reach of motels and hotels.

Economy is another reason for camping, a very valid one, and thinking of it reminds me of an incident which took place at a roadside campground in Kansas. We had stopped for the evening and had our camp made when a heavily laden station wagon bearing California license plates rolled into a site about 30 yards away.

Almost before the vehicle stopped the doors popped open, spilling out an unbelievable number of children of assorted ages. They swarmed over the luggage rack and into the rear of the wagon, and in minutes there were ten sleeping bags unrolled on tarps spread on the ground. Then the mini-army fled for the restrooms.

The couple explained to us later that night, when we visited around a campfire, that it would have been impossible for their family of ten to make the trip east to see relatives without camping. Motel and restaurant bills for man, woman, and eight children would have been prohibitive. They also explained that their rule was that nobody could visit the restroom until the bedrolls were down.

Because of the relatively low cost of travel by camping families, more people have been able to experience the wonders of our nation in the past decade than ever before. I know that the lives of our children have been enriched tremendously through outdoor living.

The overriding reason why some thirty million people participate in camping each year, however, is simply because it is fun. A hamburger charcoaled deep in the forest, beneath the sighing needles of towering trees, tastes better than one cooked in the antiseptic cleanliness of a sparkling kitchen. Man and boy grow closer together when separated by a campfire than by a television set. So do husband and wife, if the camping trip is carefully planned.

BEFORE YOU LEAP

Camping can be primitive or luxurious, but plan the first exposure of your family to camping with comfort in mind. This can be accomplished no matter how simple or complex your outing is to be.

Make that first camping experience a brief one—overnight or a weekend, perhaps. And choose a site near home, so that it is easy to return for items which you might have forgotten. The point is that you alone would simply do without, but those things might be of great importance to your wife or children.

We use such a short shakedown campout near home, sometimes in our backyard, as a preliminary to moving out on longer junkets. No matter how experienced a camper you are, it is fairly easy to forget. These shakedowns reveal shortages very quickly.

This is particularly true when you are using a new camper, trailer, tent trailer or tent—any kind of camping gear which you haven't been using. There is just no way to anticipate everything that will be needed, which leaves actual experience as the only sure guide.

CHECKLISTS

Over the years you will build up your own individual checklists for various kinds of camping trips, and these will be invaluable. Most good books on camping offer suggested lists, and you'll find one at the end of this chapter.

Few sportsmen will find need for all of the items on any such list, but from it they can select those which fit their particular situation.

When you, as a veteran sportsman-camper, first begin to take your family along, examine these camping checklists with an entirely new viewpoint. You probably won't leave out many things you formerly took on stag trips, but you'll add quite a few new ones.

PACKING FOR CAMPING

These short trial runs will sort out what you should and should not take along, but they will also help you decide where your gear should be carried. Packing is an art perfected by experience, no matter what kind of camping trip is involved.

Having enough space in your camping unit to contain everything you and your family want to take along is often a problem. You are suddenly transporting family living from a multi-room home to a much smaller space, with the obvious limitations. Two factors usually come into play to alleviate this situation.

First is that, with experience, campers learn how to pack more efficiently, and they find many more nooks and crannies in their camping unit for storage than they thought were there originally. The ingenuity of veterans of this hobby is endless, and you can learn a great deal from talking with other campers.

The second thing is that experience also teaches all of us that we can get along nicely in camp with much less gear than we first thought. On early trips we take items along "just in case," but later we do not hesitate to omit them.

PACKING—CLOTHING

Suitcases do not lend themselves well for camping use. They are bulky and awkward, and difficult to pack anywhere except in the trunk of an automobile. If your car will be with you on the camping trip, and you have no need for the trunk room for other gear, *then* suitcases may be in order.

Duffel bags are best for most situations, which is why they are used almost universally by campers. They come in all sizes, and should have a full-length zippered opening for easy access to all the contents.

Since they are made of a soft material, duffel bags pack easily. They conform to the shape space you happen to have available to quite a degree, and the space they require decreases if they are not full. Suitcases, on the other hand, require the same amount of space whether they are full or empty. Airline flight bags are nothing more than miniature duffel bags, and they are ideal for camping.

Most duffel bags are made of heavy canvas, and are available from many manufacturers. There are others available of leather, or canvas with leather trim, and there is another which we discovered in the Eddie Bauer catalog which has proved to be very useful. It is made of waterproof, flexible vinyl, comes in three sizes, and is inexpensive. Although it can be used like any other bag, we have found it perfect for transporting wet or dirty gear.

The kids have taken one more swim just before breaking camp, so what do you do with the wet swim suits en route to the next campsite? Into the waterproof duffel bag. Likewise for wet towels, muddy shoes and similar items. Taking care of the contents of this bag, of course, should be one of the first chores performed at your next stop.

Duffel bags are perfect for tent camping. They pack well in a car trunk, and handle well inside the tent. They are acceptable for camping in a tent trailer if you have room in the trunk for them. There usually is not enough room in the trailer for more than two people *and* duffel bags. In a motor home there is usually enough storage and hanging space that luggage is no problem.

For all our camping, and especially for pickup camper living, we have found that a transparent pillowcase made of plastic, which has a full-length zipper opening, fits our needs.

Like duffel bags, these cases conform to the shape of the contents. They can be used as pillows, for sleeping at night or for resting or reading during the daytime, simply by slipping over them a regular cloth pillowcase. They hold a surprising amount, and one of their most convenient features is that you can actually see the contents. One of the drawbacks of a duffel bag is the necessity to rummage around in it to locate items. With the transparent pillowcase you can look for a particular shirt, then reach directly for it. For youngsters this is a particular blessing.

In packing pillowcases or duffel bags, we have usually found it best to roll each item of clothing tightly and secure it with rubber bands. Handled in this manner they keep better through all the pulling, tugging and bouncing, and actually stay in surprisingly good condition.

Most camp clothing, particularly the stay-press kind, lends itself admirably to this kind of handling. It is practical to buy only stay-press camp clothing, with the obvious exception of woolens, down clothing and other items which don't lend themselves to this treatment.

Any dress clothing which you take along on your camping trip, if it is called for, will not fare particularly well if rolled up in a duffel bag. When we are using a pickup camper, we take such garments on hangers. Operating from a tent or a tent trailer, we usually take along one suitcase in which we carry all of the dress clothing for the family.

If your camping trip takes you into the backcountry, whether for the purpose of hunting, fishing, exploring or just for camping, you won't need dress clothes. If your camping is part of a vacation trip which involves rather extensive, repeated travel, however, you should plan for periodic stops at restaurants and motels, and that will require clothing other than camp type.

The restaurant stops give the family a change of pace from camp cooking. On our extensive camping junkets we make it a practice to spend the night in a motel now and then—once a week or twice a week, usually, depending upon where we are, what we're doing and how everybody feels about it. The motel overnight gives everybody opportunity for a bit more privacy, and it does something else. The expense of $12–$30 for the night makes you appreciate more fully the normal fee of $2–$3 at a campground.

PACKING—MISCELLANEOUS

How campers ever got along in the era B.T. (Before Tupperware) I'll never know. We did, of course, but it was with much greater difficulty than is the case now.

This versatile line of containers did not originate with camping in mind, but campers soon discovered their numerous possibilities. They came in a wide variety of shapes and sizes, with lids which were tight enough to withstand dust, water and rough treatment, and they were unbreakable.

Tupperware containers still have all of those attributes, and in recent years the manufacturer has developed the line specifically with the outdoorsman in mind. It now includes units which are useful for a wide assortment of camping and outdoor purposes.

The obvious use for these containers is for food supplies. Before leaving on a camping trip, we transfer all supplies which are packaged in boxes or bags to Tupperware containers—such things as flour, sugar, salt, cereals, eggs, coffee, cheese, bread, milk and meat.

Cardboard milk cartons will not stand a great deal of bouncing and jarring, and when they spring a leak en route the result is quite a mess in your cooler or icebox. Now we pour milk from the cartons to Tupperware beverage containers as soon as we buy it. The same is true for bread, which can quickly become squashed. A loaf of bread is difficult to keep in good condition, safe from squashing, except in a Tupperware container.

To eliminate weight, we frequently open canned goods and put them in the lightweight plastic containers. With proper cooling, juices and vegetables will keep for several days when handled in this manner.

These great camping aids are perfect for storing such things as maps and booklets, cameras and film, binoculars, games, shells and cartridges, gun-cleaning equipment, notebooks, a first-aid kit, matches and tools. Almost anything that needs protection from dust, water, dirt, bugs or bouncing is a candidate for Tupperware.

If you line the proper size Tupperware container with foam padding, which is readily available now, you can protect from breakage even very fragile items.

COOKING

As a sportsman, you already have experience at feeding yourself in the outdoors. When you begin to take your family along, however, you face a different situation.

The thing to keep in mind is that the purpose for taking your wife along is not so that she can be camp cook and dishwasher. As so many have told me, she can cook and keep house at home much more pleasantly with the modern conveniences available there.

All members of the family should participate in some way in the preparation of food and the cleanup operation. Some allocate this on a day-to-day basis, or a meal-to-meal arrangement. Some of your family may prefer to cook and others prefer to clean up. Work out a system that fits your family best.

But don't put the burden on your wife's back!

HOW TO CAMP

There are many good books available on the various kinds of camping, and all campers should have at least one or two of them. They explore the advantages and disadvantages of the different methods in great detail, and go into the mechanics of actually living in the outdoors.

Sleeping in tents is the first picture which comes to most minds when camping is mentioned. It is one of the oldest forms, and is still best in many situations, but consider that it may not be best for your family at all. It may especially not be recommended for the first exposure of your wife or youngsters to the pleasures of outdoor living.

Most women—my wife included—prefer not to sleep on the ground, even if it is inside a tent in a sleeping bag. They have an aversion to crawling creatures such as bugs or snakes, regardless of whether or not there are actually any around. That being the case, they get more rest if their bed is above ground, and preferably if their feet are above ground.

Regardless of which kind of camping you choose to do first, it is a good idea to rent your equipment for the first trip or two. Excellent gear is available in all parts of the country, through rental agencies, at quite modest prices.

For tent camping you can rent tents, sleeping bags, stoves, lanterns, coolers—the complete array. You can rent tent campers, pickup campers, trailers or motor homes. It may be desirable for you to try several of these before electing to buy your own. This would be much preferable to spending quite a sum of money on one particular kind of camping equipment and then finding it not suitable for your family. Or, worse yet, to discover that your family doesn't like camping at all.

TENT TRAILERS

It was with this in mind that I selected a tent trailer for that first, long camping vacation for my family, and in retrospect I feel that the choice was perfect. This unit consists of a metal body on two wheels, topped by a canvas canopy which folds down for traveling and up for living.

These trailers tow easily, and can be erected ready for camp use in from five to fifteen minutes. Most have foam-rubber mattresses to sleep four to six people, an icebox, storage compartments, sink and water system, and frequently a small stove.

For my family the choice, at the time, was a good one. Mary approved

Tent trailer combines comfort and the feeling of roughing it in the outdoors. Easily towed behind a car, trailer opens quickly and sleeps four to six persons on foam mattresses. Other comforts include sink, icebox and small stove.

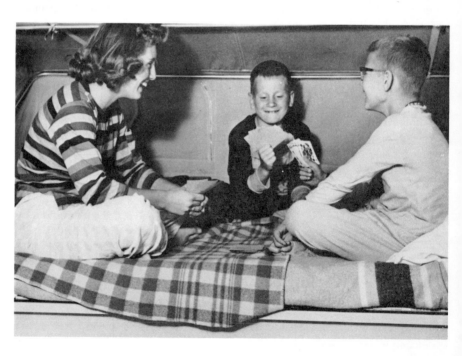

Roomy bed in the tent trailer serves as a card table to keep young people occupied when bad weather excludes outdoor activities.

64

of having our living area above ground, yet the trailer was not so civilized as to remove all aspects of camping from the trip. This latter was important for my young boys, who actually spent many nights outside the trailer in sleeping bags.

PICKUP CAMPERS

The advent of the piggyback home, a room which fits into the bed of a pickup truck, has been a boon to the wanderers of this nation. Only a couple of decades ago the sight of one of these units was unusual enough to turn heads, but now there are literally hundreds of thousands of them in use.

The pickup truck is one of the most versatile vehicles in use, and the pickup camper idea began when somebody decided to make it more versatile. He built a cover over the bed of the truck, and used the small crawl space as a protected area for his bedroll. From there the idea took wings. Simple covers are still available, and serve a purpose, but now there are also available plush units of great size and luxury.

The two general kinds of pickup campers are the slide-in units and the chassis mounts. The former are exactly what the name implies: camper units which slide into the bed of a regular pickup truck. If the owner wants to use the truck as a truck, he can remove the camper by means of jacks.

The chassis-mount unit is fitted to a pickup cab and chassis, with the truck body missing. The advantage here is that the unit can be larger, with more storage space. The disadvantage is that the vehicle is restricted to use as a camper.

In practice, surprisingly few owners of the slide-in models ever remove the camper.

As much as my family liked the tent trailer, they liked the pickup camper even more when we tried that form of camping. For the trial, an assignment from an outdoor magazine, I chose a slide-in camper manufactured by Dreamer, one of the largest of the many camper builders. We used a slide-in unit since that is the most popular style.

Our assignment trip would take us through the Southwest and extensively through Mexico. With much rugged off-highway travel in prospect, I mounted the camper on a 4-wheel-drive Jeep Gladiator truck. There were not many occasions when the 4-wheel-drive feature was needed, but on those few it was invaluable.

Our camper was fairly average, so a description of it will indicate what a camper is and does. We had one full-size double bed in the over-the-cab extension, and two more bunks which became mini-double beds in slide-out fashion. All had foam mattresses.

The camper had an icebox (butane refrigerators are optional), gas stove, gas heater, dinette table, sink and pressure water system, and a combination toilet and shower stall. We had an intercom system for communicating between camper and cab.

If additional sleeping space isn't needed, most families would find a sleep-four arrangement best, since this will permit additional built-ins for storage.

There was a time when the expression "drives like a truck" was not a very complimentary term, but no more. Our Jeep pickup had comfortable, deep-foam bucket seats, power steering and power brakes, automatic transmission (unusual with 4-wheel-drive), air conditioning, radio (which could be piped into the camper via the intercom), and a powerful 250 horsepower engine. My wife and our eighteen-year-old daughter handled it with ease and enjoyment.

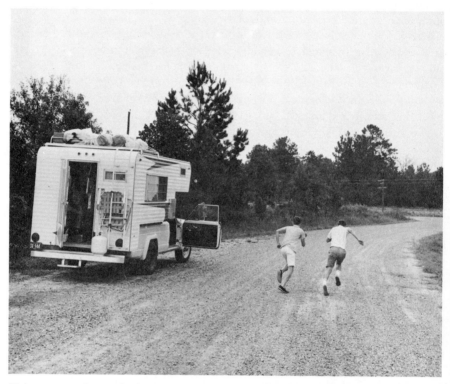

Pickup camper is popular for family camping. It contains all the comforts of a tent trailer, plus toilet and shower. Truck drives easily and is equipped with power brakes and steering. An occasional stop gives boys a chance to expend excess energy.

The advantage of a pickup camper over a towed unit is that it can go almost anywhere the truck could go, and that does not exclude many places. Once in Mexico we were stymied by a tunnel through a mountain which would not permit passage of the camper, but on other occasions we did negotiate sharp turns and twists which would not have been possible pulling a trailer of any kind.

A disadvantage of the pickup camper is that your living quarters and your transportation are one and the same. If you range out from a campsite for sightseeing, fishing, hunting or shopping, you must take your home with you.

There is a new unit on the market which may eliminate this disadvantage for some. It's the Jeep camper, which is a hybrid between a towed travel trailer and a pickup camper. It attaches to any 4-wheel-drive Jeep Universal vehicle, and has a set of wheels of its own. In camp the unit can be unhooked, and the Jeep used as a separate vehicle.

One innovation of some regular pickup campers is a walk-through or crawl-through between the pickup cab and the camper itself. It permits movement back and forth while in transit, although only for the very agile in the case of the crawl-through, but is has other advantages.

The opening allows those riding in the camper to furnish the cab occupants with food and drink, and allows parents riding up front to keep a closer eye on youngsters in the rear. It also allows cool air from an air-conditioned cab to flow back into the camper.

Children find traveling in a pickup camper much more enjoyable, because it is less confining, than when they must ride in an automobile. It is similar to traveling in a home, and our girl and boys took turns sleeping, eating, drinking, reading, sight-seeing and playing games.

Mary and I, too, if the truth be known, found it more enjoyable. We did essentially the same things while Barbara was driving, and I even managed to get some writing done while in transit.

One item which we found valuable in our pickup camper was a portable ice chest. It gave us additional space for ice and perishables, served as a step-up to the cab-over space, and was a convenient place to keep cold drinks. The door of the regular icebox built into the camper should be bolted shut while the camper is on the move, otherwise it may jar open and spill the contents.

An optional item which we ordered with our camper was a sundeck, and a ladder leading up to it. The purpose for having it was to gain additional storage room, particularly for bulky items which were not used regularly. Included in the array of equipment which we carried on it were tackle boxes, golf clubs, sleeping bags and a tent.

Why take a tent when you have sleeping accommodations inside? No matter how patient and considerate the members of a family are, the environs of a pickup camper are confining for four or five people. When we felt the urge or the need, we just pitched our Pop-Tent at the campsite alongside the camper. Anybody who wanted to have a bit more privacy for the night appropriated the tent.

Having the extra sleeping—or storage—room of a tent is particularly useful when you stay at one campsite for several days. Another advantage is that the tent serves notice, when you are out sight-seeing or shopping in the camper, that your campsite is occupied.

The tent, the portable ice chest, a one-burner Coleman stove we carried, a thermos jug of water and several lawn chairs made a fairly complete camp in itself. This was an advantage when I needed the camper to sneak off to a nearby fishing stream.

MOTOR HOMES

The ultimate in luxury is found in these rolling homes. They are just about that—plush living quarters built on a special chassis.

These units, in their finest form, are really apartments with all the conveniences. Most have facilities for sleeping, dining, cooking, sanitation, bathing (hot and cold running water), lighting and air conditioning. They have abundant storage room for clothes, kitchen equipment, and hobby gear. They usually cost from $8,000 to $12,000.

Many of these resemble multi-passenger buses, and indeed some of them started out that way. The driver's seat is inside the home, just as is the bus driver's seat on a regular passenger bus.

A trend in this type of unit is toward motor homes of more modest proportions and appointments, which brings the cost down and makes them available to more families. Sale of motor homes overall has been increasing at a surprising rate in the past year or two, and these smaller units are accounting for a substantial portion of the total.

One of the limitations of the motor home is that it is not a backwoods unit. In general, its use must be restricted to the paved highways, since the low road clearance and long wheelbase don't permit travel on rough roads. Also, most people are reluctant to take a $10,000 unit too far from civilization.

TRAVEL TRAILERS

These have been around for a long time, but modern developments have left their mark here in the form of lighter and stronger construction, and in better equipment inside. Trailers can be as big and as luxurious as your tastes and pocketbook prefer or permit.

For vacation use, of course, the big mobile homes are not practical. Sportsmen should stick to units which are smaller—in the Airstream size range, since these can be towed readily with the average passenger automobile, and because they will fit into many campground trailer sites which will not accommodate larger units.

As with the tent campers, another advantage here is that the towing vehicle is free to be used for other purposes once camp is established—once the trailer is parked.

TENTS

There was a time when tents were drab, heavy, bulky and very hard to erect. There are still some which fit into this category, but the revolution in camping equipment of the past decade has resulted in something better. Now you have a choice of many styles, colors and materials.

Tent materials, in a variety of bright colors as well as in the traditional green or brown, include nylon, Dacron, lighter-weight canvas, drills and other synthetics. The newer materials are light in weight, and are surprisingly durable.

Quickly erected Pop tent, carried on the camper roof, gives added sleeping and storage space in a semipermanent camp.

Modern tents often have outside aluminum framework, instead of interior poles, to hold them up. This system eliminates obstructions inside the tent.

Tarp provides a protected area for cooking and dining. Many tents have a canopy in front of the door which serves the same purpose.

Tent framing is now largely made of aluminum or fiberglass, and the tent designs permit most of them to be erected easily.

The tent you choose for your family, regardless of which style you choose, should have a *waterproof*, sewed-in floor. It is preferable that this waterproof floor material extend up the walls of the tent a few inches.

The material of the tent itself, keep in mind, is actually water repellent rather than being waterproof. This permits it to breathe.

In all tent camping, but especially when you have your family along, it is helpful to erect an additional covered area outside the tent. Many tents have a canopy which protects the space immediately in front of the tent door, but you can easily fashion more living room by stretching a tarp between trees or poles. This outside protected area is almost a necessity for cooking and dining, and provides a lounge for periods other than mealtimes.

BACKPACKING

This is a specialized form of camping, one which is not generally best for the beginner. Few sportsmen, in other words, should choose this kind of outing for their families until they have had some experience in other forms.

70

Equipment for backpack camping has been refined to an amazing degree in recent years. One outfitter, for instance, sells a 20-pound pack which includes tent, sleeping bag, foam pad, down vest, rain poncho, aluminum kettle set, grille, plastic mug, knife-fork-spoon, flashlight and almost 5 pounds of freeze-dried foods. (Gerry, P. O. Box 5544 Denver, Colorado 80217.)

GROUP CAMPING

It is often much more fun to take a camping trip with friends. Many families make it a practice to vacation with another family, which has advantages for both adults and children. Not only is the actual trip itself fun, but getting together to plan these outings furnishes an additional recreational benefit.

One of the fondest memories of my childhood is of our summer camping trips. For years several families in my town established a rather permanent camp at a site on a lake not more than 30 miles from home. Two large army pyramid tents formed the backbone of the camp, with assorted other shelters coming and going as the need arose.

The occupants of our camp varied from week to week as one family would come, another go. The children of most of the families spent most of the summer

If your family enjoys horseback riding, there is no greater thrill than a pack trip in the western mountains. This was base camp for pack outfit in Montana wilderness area.

at this camp, being cared for by the adults who happened to be in occupancy at the moment. It was a wonderful way to spend a vacation.

One of the most frequent sights along highways and at campgrounds and resorts today is the pair of pickup campers, or the pair of tent trailers, or the pair of travel trailers. They represent two couples or families who are friends back home, and who take this opportunity to spend their vacations together. It may not be two couples from the same town for that matter, since a camping trip of this kind is a wonderful way for people who live in different parts of the country to get together.

Traveling in pairs like this or in groups of campers does have advantages. That fourth for bridge is always available. Wives can visit and babysit while the men do men-type things. And, conversely, men can visit and babysit while the wives shop or sight-see.

Another advantage is that one of the couples can babysit all the children while the other couple hunts, fishes, or just takes a walk to get away by themselves for a while.

Couples or families which camp together can coordinate their camping gear to great advantage. If the meals are prepared and eaten together, then one salt shaker obviously is enough. This line of reasoning can be carried throughout the list of camping equipment. Each family will be able to take along less gear yet have more available for use.

The additional manpower in that other pickup camper or in that other tent is most welcome in a deer camp. When you have a big buck down in a deep ravine, it is quite an advantage to have another man around, especially if he has a few strong healthy youngsters. Any emergency situation, such as the prospect of being snowed in, increases the value of group camping.

ACTIVITIES—PLAN AHEAD

No matter what kind of camping trip you are planning, try to anticipate the opportunities for recreation which exist at that particular site. What's available? Fishing? Hunting? Sight-seeing? Bird watching?

The best way to get such information is to write to the agencies which administer fish and game, and which are responsible for tourist promotion. In some states these may be one and the same, but in most they are two separate agencies. These agencies have a great deal of material outlining the recreational possibilities in their states. When you write, request any information which might be of value to a vacationing tourist. If you have special interests be sure to mention them.

Make it a point to take along appropriate books, no matter what kind of camping trip is involved. Some of the standard field books which are part of our equipment most of the time—one of Roger Tory Peterson's field books of birds; *Field Book of Snakes*, by Schmidt and Davis; *North American Game Fishes*, by La-Monte; *Field Book of Marine Fishes*, by Breder; and *The Mammal Guide*, by Palmer. In addition to these there are many specialized books and pamphlets on such things as insects, flowers, shrubs, seashells and other facets of nature.

Make it a practice, when traveling, to stop at the tourist welcome stations which most states maintain at their borders. These usually have the latest information about road conditions, camping areas and tourist attractions in that particular state.

PESTS AND POISONOUS PLANTS

The outdoors is not normally a caressing, inviting environment for people. It is frequently harsh and uninviting, resisting the efforts of the camper to enjoy himself. Sportsmen enjoy the outdoors in spite of these discomforts, but with the family along they must make a special effort to smooth out the rough spots, and to minimize the discomfort. They must certainly guard against any of the dangers which might be encountered on a particular trip.

Insects are the most frequent, persistent and annoying of the pests with which campers must contend. The methods of coping with insects are generally three in number: keep them out, repel them or kill them.

Most important is that you have bug-free sleeping quarters on your camping trip. Modern tents, tent trailers, campers and trailers are insectproof to a substantial degree. Tents have sewed-in floors, screened windows and a zipper closure for the door which will keep out most bugs. If insects are present in the area, particularly mosquitos, some will get into your living quarters during the day as people enter and leave. If this happens, spray the interior for a few seconds with a good insecticide bomb before bedtime. Stay outside until the fumes dissipate.

Never go on a camping trip without one of the good insect repellents such as Cutters, 6-12 or Off. Apply as directed to exposed skin, and particularly to the cuffs of trousers or around the legs, wherever ticks, mosquitos or chiggers are found. That means just about everywhere.

There are only four kinds of poisonous snakes in this country. They are the rattlesnake, copperhead, water moccasin and coral snake, and one or more of these species is found in most parts of the nation.

Despite this, the odds of your encountering one of these poisonous snakes are quite small. Although the prospect of snakebite is fearful and spectacular, the danger to your family is infinitely greater while you are traveling on the highways.

Regardless of the small odds, however, teach your family to respect the possibility of snakebite. Chances are good that you as a sportsman already own a snakebite kit. If not, get one and teach your family how to use it.

Keep in mind that the best treatment for snakebite is to get the victim to a doctor as soon as possible. The use of that snake-bite kit is an emergency measure, but one which may have to be employed if you are in the back country.

Poisonous snakes are not vicious and want only to be left alone. They fear people fully as much as people fear them and much prefer to hide or escape rather than to fight. The greatest danger for an outdoorsman is to approach a snake unexpectedly, or in such a situation that the snake cannot escape.

Teach your family that they must be more careful about where they put their hands and feet when in the outdoors than is necessary back in town. Don't step over logs without looking to see what's on the other side. When climbing, don't reach for handholds on the ledge above unless you can see that it is free of snakes. When wandering around the campground after dark, always use a light.

Contrary to popular belief, snakes are not slimy. They are clean and interesting creatures and most of them are very beneficial. Bee stings are much more of a problem to the average outdoors family than are poisonous snakes. More people actually die from the stings of wasps, yellowjackets, honey bees and hornets than die from poisonous snakebites.

The real danger from bees is from stumbling into a concentration of them where you might receive multiple stings. Be alert to avoid such situations. If you are bitten or stung, the immediate application of ice or ice water is helpful in giving relief. Also good is a paste made of baking soda and cold cream or a compress soaked with ammonia water. A strong alcohol solution or calamine lotion is helpful in relieving the itching.

Contact with poisonous plants is something all outdoor people must contend with and guard against. Although exposure to one of these plants may not be serious, the discomfort can be great and a vacation trip can be ruined.

The three plants to watch out for are the common poison ivy, poison oak, poison sumac. Poison ivy grows everywhere in the United States with the exception of California and possibly some of the adjacent states. Poison oak is found only in California and the other western states, while poison sumac is found in most of the eastern third of the United States. Teach your family to identify these plants.

Poison ivy may be in the form of either a vine or a shrub; poison oak usually appears as a bundle or a clump of plants with many stems rising from one root system. It is called poison oak because the leaves resemble those of an oak tree. The leaflets of both poison ivy and poison oak are their most distinguishing feature, since there are always three of them.

Poison sumac is a woody shrub or a small tree—never a vine. Found especially in low swampy areas, it has from seven to thirteen leaflets which in the spring are bright orange. Later on these leaflets assume the same color as those of poison ivy and poison oak, which is a dark glossy green above and a pale green on the underside.

Treatment for exposure to one of these poisonous plants is to wash the part with soap and water as soon as possible, then to sponge it off with alcohol. Again, calamine lotion is usually soothing.

Tourists who visit such national parks as Yellowstone and Smoky Mountain will frequently see bears. They are interesting to watch, but keep in mind that these are wild animals, no matter how tame they seem. Treat them as wild animals which are potentially dangerous. If you photograph them, which most of us do, do so at a distance. By all means follow the park service regulations against feeding these animals.

WHERE TO CAMP

There are many campgrounds in this country and in Canada, but the problem of the camper is to find one suitable campground in the right place when he needs it. The best way is to utilize one of the many guides that are available.

Guides we have used with satisfaction, include: from Rand McNally (edited by Barcam Publishing Company, Box F, Palos Verdes Peninsula, California 90274)—*Guidebook to Campgrounds,* listing more than 12,000 U.S. and Canadian campgrounds having over 450,000 campsites, and *Travel Trailer Guide*; from Woodall Publishing Company, 500 Hyacinth Place, Hyland Park, Illinois 60035, *Woodall's Trailering Parks and Campgrounds,* a comprehensive listing of more than 10,000 privately owned campgrounds, plus an assortment of other valuable camping information; from Camping Maps, U.S.A., Box 2034, Palos Verdes Peninsula, California 90274—*Private Campgrounds, U.S.A.* and *Overnight Trailer Parks; Camping Maps, Canada* and *Boat Camping Maps, U.S.A.*

Other guides which we have found useful are Rand-McNally's *Vacation Guide,* which lists more than 2,500 points of interest in the U.S., Canada and Mexico; Rand-McNally's *Golf Course Guide,* a state-by-state directory of more than 5,000 golf courses; and Rand-McNally's *The National Park Guide,* which covers all thirty-two national parks and which will greatly increase the pleasure which your family derives from visiting one of them.

Maps and lists of campgrounds are available from many federal agencies, including the National Park Service, the U.S. Forest Service, the Bureau of Land Management and the Army Corps of Engineers. Write to these agencies in Washington, D.C. for information.

A rather new development in the private campground field is the formation of chains of campgrounds. The largest of these and one of the best is Kampgrounds of America, recognized by its symbol KOA. It has more than a hundred affiliates from coast to coast and more are being added each month. One feature of the KOA system is a free reservation service which enables a camper to move from one KOA campground to another with assurance that he will have a space when he gets there. A directory of campgrounds affiliated with KOA is available from Post Office Box 1138, Billings, Montana 59103.

Campers who live in big cities can usually find all of their equipment in local stores. Those who are from smaller towns, however, may need to utilize the catalog houses. Some of the better known ones from which you can get free catalogs by writing are Eddie Bauer, 417 East Pine Street, Seattle, Washington 98122; L. L. Bean, Inc., Freeport, Maine 04032; I. Goldberg, 902 Chestnut Street, Philadelphia, Pennsylvania 19107; Klein's Sporting Goods, 227 West Washington Street, Chicago, Illinois 60606; The Orvis Company, Manchester, Vermont 05254; Moor and Mountain, Concord, Massachusetts 01742 (which specializes in lightweight camping equipment); Morsan, 810 Route 17, Paramus, New Jersey 07652; Himalayan Equipment (which specializes in backpacking equipment); Bear Archery Company, Grayling, Michigan 49738; Sears Roebuck and Company; and Montgomery Ward.

STATE SOURCES OF CAMPING INFORMATION

ALABAMA—Dept. of Conservation, Montgomery 36104

ALASKA—Fish and Wildlife Service, Juneau 99801
   Div. of Econ. & Tourist Development, Juneau 99801

ARIZONA—Game & Fish Comm., Phoenix 85007

ARKANSAS—Game & Fish Comm., Little Rock 72201
   Arkansas Pub. & Parks Comm., Little Rock 72201

CALIFORNIA—Dept. of Fish & Game, Sacramento 95814
   Dept. of Natural Resources, Sacramento 95814

COLORADO—Game, Fish & Parks Dept., Denver 80216
   Dept. of Public Relations, Denver 80216

CONNECTICUT—State Development Comm., Hartford 06115

DELAWARE—Delaware State Development Dept., Dover 19901

DISTRICT OF COLUMBIA—Washington Con. & Vis. Bureau, Washington 20001
   National Parks Association, Washington 20001
   National Capital Parks, Washington 20001

FLORIDA—Game & Fresh Water Fish Comm., Tallahassee 32304
   Florida Devel. Comm., Tallahassee 32304

GEORGIA—State Game & Fish Comm., Atlanta 30334
   Georgia Dept. of Commerce, Atlanta 30334
   Dept. of State Parks, Atlanta 30334

HAWAII—Hawaii Visitors Bureau, Honolulu 96813

IDAHO—Dept. of Fish & Game, Boise 83707
   State Dept. of Comm. & Devel., Boise 83707

ILLINOIS—Dept. of Conservation, Springfield 62706

INDIANA—Dept. of Conservation, Indianapolis 46204
   Dept. of Comm. & Pub. Rel., Indianapolis 46204

IOWA—State Conservation Comm., Des Moines
  Iowa Development Comm., Des Moines

KANSAS—Kansas Indus. Devel. Comm., Topeka
   Forestry, Fish & Game Comm., Pratt 67124

KENTUCKY—Kentucky Dept. of Pub. Rel., Frankfort 40601
   Kentucky Tourist & Travel Comm., Frankfort 40601

LOUISIANA—Wildlife & Fisheries Comm., New Orleans 70130
   Tourist Comm., Baton Rouge

MAINE—Dept. of Inland Fisheries & Game, Augusta 04430
   Maine Publicity Bureau Gateway Circle, Portland

MARYLAND—Game & Inland Fish Comm., Annapolis 21404
   Dept. of Information, Annapolis 21404

MASSACHUSETTS—Div. of Fisheries & Game, Boston 02202
   Dept. of Commerce, Boston 02202

MICHIGAN—Michigan Tourist Council, Lansing 48926
   Dept. of Conservation, Lansing 48926
MINNESOTA—Div. of Promotion & Publ., St. Paul 55101
   State Parks Div., St. Paul 55101
   Div. of Game & Fish, St. Paul 55101
MISSISSIPPI—Game & Fish Comm., Jackson 39205
   Mississippi Park Comm., Jackson 39205
   Mississippi Agric. & Indus. Bd., Jackson 39205
MISSOURI—Missouri Div. of Res. & Devel., Jefferson City 65101
MONTANA—Montana Fish and Game Dept., Helena 59601
   State Highway Comm., Helena 59601
NEBRASKA—Nebraska Game, Forestation & Parks Comm., Lincoln 68509
NEVADA—Nevada Dept. of Econ. Devel., Carson City
   Fish & Game Comm., Reno 89510
NEW HAMPSHIRE—Fish & Game Dept., Concord 03301
   New Hampshire State Plan. & Devel. Comm.,
    Concord 03301
NEW JERSEY—Div. of Fish & Game, Trenton 08625
   Dept. of Conservation & Economic Development, Trenton
    08625
NEW MEXICO—Dept. of Game & Fish, Santa Fe 87501
   New Mexico Dept. of Devel., Santa Fe 87501
NEW YORK—State Dept. of Commerce, Albany 12226
   New York Fish & Game, Albany 12226
NORTH CAROLINA—Wildlife Resources Comm., Raleigh 27602
   Dept. of Conservation & Development, Raleigh 27602
NORTH DAKOTA—State Game & Fish Dept., Bismarck 58501
   N.D. State Highway Comm., Bismarck 58501
OHIO—Dept. of National Resources, Columbus 43212
   Ohio Develop. & Pub. Comm., Columbus 43212
OKLAHOMA—Dept. of Wildlife Conservation, Oklahoma City 73105
OREGON—State Game Comm., Portalnd 97201
   Travel Information Div., Salem
PENNSYLVANIA—State Dept. of Forests & Waters, Harrisburg 17120
   Bureau of Travel Devel., Harrisburg 17120
RHODE ISLAND—Div. of Fish & Game, Providence 02903
   Information Division, Providence 02903
   Publicity & Recreation Div., Providence 02903
SOUTH CAROLINA—South Carolina Devel. Board, Columbia 29209
   Wildlife Resources Comm., Columbia 29209
SOUTH DAKOTA—Dept. of Game, Fish & Parks, Pierre 57501
   State Highway Comm., Pierre 57501

TENNESSEE—Dept. of Conservation, Nashville 37203
        Game & Fish Comm., Nashville 37203
        Div. of State Parks, Nashville 37203

TEXAS—Texas Hwy. Dept., Austin 78701
        Parks & Wildlife Comm., Austin 78701

UTAH—Utah Tour. & Pub. Council, Salt Lake City 84116
        Dept. of Fish & Game, Salt Lake City 84116
        Tourist & Publicity Council, Salt Lake City 84116

VERMONT—Vermont Devel. Comm., Montpelier 05602
        Department of Forest & Parks, Montpelier 05602

VIRGINIA—Div. of Public Rel. & Adv., Richmond 23213
        Div. of Parks, Richmond 23213

WASHINGTON—Wash. State Dept. of Comm., Olympia 98501
        Dept. of Game, Olympia 98501
        State Resort Assn., Seattle
        Dept. of Commerce & Economic Dev., Olympia 98501

WEST VIRGINIA—W. Va. Indus. & Pub. Comm., Charleston 25305
        Conservation Comm., Charleston 25305

WISCONSIN—Conservation Dept., Madison 53701

WYOMING—Wyoming Travel Comm., Cheyenne 82001
        Game & Fish Comm., Cheyenne 82001

PUERTO RICO—Puerto Rico Visitors Bureau, San Juan

VIRGIN ISLANDS—Tourist Development Board, St. Thomas
        Virgin Islands National Park, St. Thomas

CAMPING CHECKLIST

Few campers will ever need all of the items on this list at any one time, but a review of it may help you keep from forgetting some essentials. Add to it things which may fit your particular situation and needs.

Basic Equipment

Tent	Rucksack
Tent Poles	Plastic Sheeting
Tent Stakes	Leveling Blocks
Tent Ropes	Battery Charger
Extra Rope	Hydraulic Jack
Tarp or Fly	Sleeping Bags
Groundcloth	Sheets
Canopy Enclosure	Blankets
Mosquito Netting	Pillows/Cases
Folding Shovel	Air Mattresses
Knife	Air Mattress Pump
Hatchet or Ax	Repair Kit
Hammer or Mallet	Cots

Twine
Canvas Repair Sewing Awl
Whisk Broom
Portable Heater
Handsaw
Poncho
Waterproofing Compound
Guy Line Adapters
Kerosene Lantern
Carbide Lamp
Coleman Type Lantern
Mantles and Generators
Lantern Pole

Hammocks
Clock
Foam Pad
File
Sharpening Stone
Flashlights
Battery Lantern
Extra Batteries
Candles
Matches
Extension Cord
Plug-in Light
Candle Lantern

Kitchen Gear

Large Frying Pan
Small Frying Pan
Large Pot
Small Pot
Dutch Oven
Plates
Bowls
Coffeepot
Drinking Cups
Griddle
Toaster
Water Bottle, Plastic
Paper Plates
Spatula
Ladle
Cooking Forks/Spoons
Serving Forks/Spoons
Eating Utensils
Bottle Opener
Can Opener
Ice Pick
Kitchen Fly/Tarp
Oilcloth
Fly Swatter
Tupperware
Cooler
Thermos
Water Container
Canteens
Picnic Basket
Wax Paper
Aluminum Foil

Wiener Forks
Pot & Pan Lifter
Plastic Bags
Stove and Fuel
Stove Stand
Stove Oven
Funnel
Firewood
Charcoal
Grill
Matches
Newspaper
Fire Starter
Waterproof Match Box
Fuel Can
Safari Grill
Pot Holders
Napkins
Tablecloth
Folding Table
Folding Chairs
Plastic Food Wrap
Salt/Pepper Shakers
Plastic Egg Box
Butter Container
Cooler Bottles
Soap/Detergent
Dish Cloths
Dish Towels
Pot Cleaners
Wash Pan
Paper Towels
Paper Sacks

Health Equipment

- Medicines
- Portable Toilet
- Extra Bags
- Toilet Tissue
- First Aid Kit
- Band Aids
- Suntan Lotion
- Snakebite Kit
- Insect Repellent
- Insect Bite Medication
- Insect Bomb
- Insect Headnet
- Halazone Tablets

Personal Care

- Washcloths
- Towels
- Soap
- Shampoo
- Washbasin
- Disposable Tissues
- Sanitary Napkins
- Toothbrushes
- Toothpaste
- Shaving Gear
- Cosmetics
- Mirror
- Manicure Kit
- Sunglasses
- Wash 'n Dri

Clothing

- Raingear
- Swim Suits
- Sweaters
- Caps or Hats
- Gloves
- Extra Shoes
- Beach Sandals
- Overshoes
- Shoelaces
- Handkerchiefs
- Belts
- Socks/Stockings
- Outer Clothing
- Underclothes
- Coat Hangers
- Sewing Kit
- Laundry Bag
- Clothesline
- Clothespins
- Hip Boots
- Waders

Recreation

- Deck of Cards
- Games
- Play Balls
- Fishing Gear
- Hunting Gear
- Hiking Gear
- Books
- Radio
- Binoculars
- Cameras/Film
- Badminton Set
- Archery Gear

Miscellaneous

- Pencil and Notebooks
- Camping Guides
- Road Maps
- Tour Books
- Equipment Spare Parts
- Tool Kit
- Emergency Whistle
- Compass

5 Boating

THE AVAILABILITY of water is the overriding factor in the choice of most Americans when they decide where they will spend their vacation. It has a substantial bearing on the location of a site for home building, and particularly, on the location for retirement homes. Water activities, then, loom large in the recreation picture of this nation.

The opportunity for water recreation in this nation, happily, is improving all the time. Thousands of ponds, small lakes and huge reservoirs have been constructed throughout the length and breadth of this nation, many in areas which were almost devoid of water recreation. That trend continues, as state, federal and private agencies move to harness the water resources of the nation for recreational, industrial and domestic uses.

It isn't necessary to boat of course to enjoy lakes and streams, but the use of some type of craft opens the door to so many more pleasures than are available to the shorebound sportsman. Boating is a distinct pleasure in itself, but then there are the other activities such as water skiing, swimming from boats, fishing and boat camping. There are many other related activities which can be enjoyed on the water, such as photography and bird watching. For you, the sportsman, one of the nicest things about this whole picture is that boating is perhaps the easiest of the outdoor activities in which to interest your wife. I have seen very few children who need cajoling, since most of them are enthusiastic from the beginning.

It's usually quite easy to get your wife into a boat the first time, but it might be much more difficult to arrange a repeat performance unless you observe certain precautions on that first one. Make sure she is comfortable both physically and mentally. It is natural for most women to be a bit fearful of boats when they are first exposed to them and it is probable that your wife will follow this pattern. Be aware of this possibility and be prepared to allay those fears by adequately explaining all phases of the boating experience which you hope she will enjoy.

Make sure that first outing is not too arduous physically. Just how you do this will depend largely upon the type of boating which is involved. Regardless of the kind, however, one cardinal rule applies: keep it short.

Comfort is the key word in family boating activities, just as it is in any family outdoor participation. If your wife and youngsters are uncomfortable, they will not be happy for very long. If they are not happy, chances are that that particular outdoor recreation will end in frustration for all.

Coast Guard-approved life preservers include, from left to right: boat cushion; yoke-type unicellular foam vest; yoke-type kapok-filled vest; ring buoy.

WATER SAFETY

When you begin taking your family afloat, one of your foremost concerns should be for their safety. Regardless of the size of the boat, there is always the possibility of falling from the boat or having the boat capsize. The members of your family should be prepared for both eventualities and schooled to cope with them.

Federal and state laws, in general, require that there be aboard any watercraft an approved life preserver for each person on board. Approved, in this case, means approval by the U.S. Coast Guard and all approved items will bear a tag designating this. The approved preservers used by most boaters are in the form of life jackets or buoyant boat cushions. Ring buoys are also on the approved list, but for obvious reasons are not practical for boating.

Water safety measures were discussed in the chapter on fishing, but some of them bear repeating here. The overriding point which must be remembered, is that a life preserver is of no value if it is beyond the reach of the person in trouble. One stored in the bow compartment of a boat, for instance, is worthless in the event of a sudden crisis. So is a boat cushion which sails off in the darkness when a boat overturns.

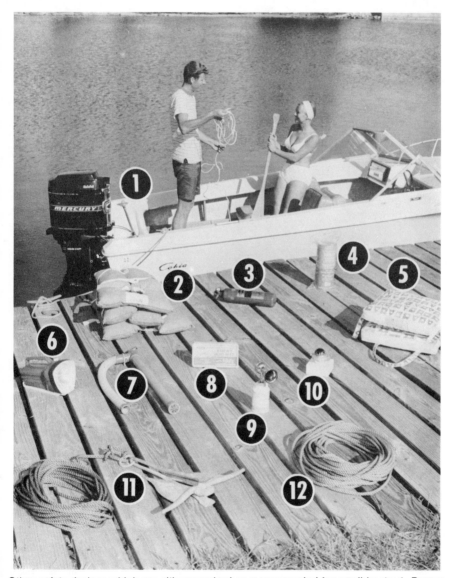

Other safety devices which are either required or recommended for small boats: 1. Proper running lights. 2. Life jackets for each person. 3. Fire extinguisher. 4. Distress signal kit. 5. Boat cushions. 6. Lantern. 7. Bilge pump. 8. First-aid kit. 9. Air horn. 10. Compass. 11. Anchor and line. 12. Extra line.

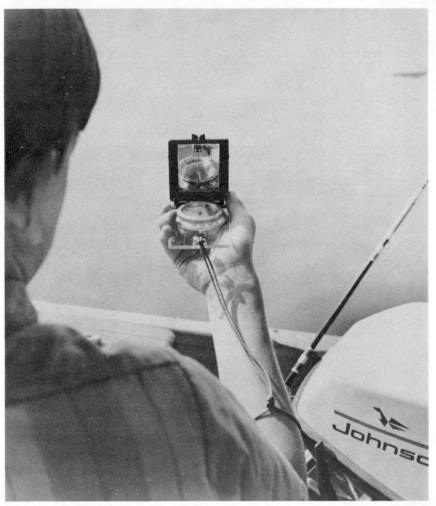

Compass is a valuable boating aid. It is used to read maps, to take bearings on the water from a sea chart and to relocate fishing spots.

If your wife or youngsters cannot swim, make sure they *wear* a life-saving device of some kind at all times when they are afloat.

All members of a sportsman's family should be able to swim. This is particularly true, of course, if your favorite hobbies include such water-connected activities as boating and fishing.

Confidence in just about anything is born of knowledge and experience, and nowhere is this more true than with boating. When they were quite young, we began teaching our youngsters the things which might possibly happen to them around water. As soon as they could swim, we deliberately overturned our small aluminum boat with all of us aboard. Barbara, Tom and Kent learned the sensation of tipping over and of finding themselves in the water with the capsized boat.

We practiced supporting ourselves in the water by holding hands across the top of an overturned boat. They learned to right the capsized craft and were surprised to find that it would support them in the water, even when completely swamped. They learned the proper way to climb back into a righted craft without tipping it over again.

We practiced falling from boats. I am positive that toppling unexpectedly from a boat would not alarm either of my youngsters since they have done it many times. As they grew older, tipping a boat over and playing on and around it became one of their favorite pastimes. Our overturned boat serves nicely as a swimming raft.

Falling out of a boat can happen to anyone. Years ago Mary and I were heading out on a fishing trip, Mary operating the outboard while I was perched precariously on the bow taking photographs. When the bow of the boat was kicked sideways by contact with an underwater stump, I rolled out sideways into 10 feet of water.

A half-dozen years later, I returned the favor. On that occasion I was running my Bass Boat too fast from the bow seat, when I hit an unexpected crosswave. The jolt pitched Mary into the water. In neither dunking was there any panic. Since we had been there before, we knew what to expect.

FUN IN A FISHING BOAT

Boats come in a staggering array of sizes and shapes, and you should keep in mind that any boat can afford a great deal of pleasure for your family. A large yacht is a thing of beauty and a family joy, but most of us must be content with more modest equipment.

When spending the day on the water, it's good idea to divide aquatic activities so all members of the family have a chance to participate. If children have their share of swimming, they'll be patient while you fish.

Allowing youngsters to handle important chores increases their self-reliance and gives the sportsman's wife more leisure. This young man was assigned the task of preparing the noon meal on a Sterno stove.

Even the average fishing boat can serve many roles in outdoor recreation. Simply paddling a boat is great fun to most youngsters, and they aren't concerned with the kind of boat it happens to be. Wives are not as prone in that direction, and I have had an unusually difficult time in finding a paddle which will fit Mary's hands, but I can recall many of our outings when Tom, Kent and Barbara occupied themselves for long periods of time just paddling our fishing boat around the area. Resign yourself to the fact that you probably won't get much fishing done during these periods, but be cheered by the prospect that you may be building for your later years some very expert boat paddlers.

It constantly surprises me that more people don't realize that they can use their small fishing outboards for water sports. Many fishing boats, powered by motors of only 10 horsepower, will pull youngsters on water skis, and even 3 to 5 horsepower outboards are great for towing the youngsters on discs and surfboards.

Whether you own your own boat or whether you rent one at the lakeside marina, keep in mind these related aquatic activities which you and your family can enjoy. You may find, as we frequently do, that it's an advantage to split your recreation day into more than one part. Perhaps you will want to spend part of it fishing, part boating and part just loafing. The results are often happier for all than if the entire day has been devoted to one purpose.

Early in her boating-fishing career, Mary brought it pointedly to my attention that most small fishing boats are uncomfortable largely because of one reason: the seats have no backrest. Portable boat seats with such backrests are available almost everywhere, and we quickly acquired a pair of these. I soon discovered that she was quite right and I rapidly became a boat seat fan myself.

Another luxury not normally associated with small boats is a canopy of some sort for protection against the sun. It actually requires only a moderate amount of ingenuity and effort to rig up a collapsible shelter which can be erected on just about any boat when needed. Ready-made folding canopies are available for most boats, of course.

Boating and cruising, simply for the sake of boating and cruising, are great activities for the outdoor enthusiast, but they may leave a great deal to be desired on the part of your youngsters. There are other things which can keep them occupied while boating, however, and some of the things which we did with our youngsters when they were little may give you some ideas.

One of the greatest "baby-sitters" which Mary discovered for our daughter Barbara during our early fishing trips before we added the two boys, was an inexpensive color book and a set of watercolors. Water was no problem, of course. Barbara just dipped her brush over the side of the boat. Water pistols kept our youngsters occupied for long periods of time. After all, the ammunition is right there and who really minds being wet when on a boating outing?

Eating and sleeping are two of the favorite pastimes of young boys and girls and this is true when they are afloat as well as when they are ashore. We always made it a point, and still do, to take along the necessary ingredients for eating and frequently for sleeping as well. A plastic sack full of snacks can break the monotony of a fishing morning which can seem interminably long to youngsters. I must say that I seldom resist the invitation to "have a bite."

We also use our boats as a base from which to camp, to picnic, to hike, to bird watch and to sight-see. Just a little bit of thought will bring home to you just how these activities can fit into the boating scheme of your family.

THE BOATING BOOM

Boating has certainly become one of the largest family participation sports in the nation, and just a few figures bring this home graphically. In 1968, the latest year for which we have figures, it is estimated that more than two million people in this country participated in recreational boating more than once or twice. They spent more than three billion dollars for new and used boats, motors, accessories, safety equipment, fuel, insurance, docking, maintenance, launching, storage, repairs and club memberships. In that year of 1968, the estimated number of recreational boats in use in the United States was a staggering 8,440,000, a dramatic increase from 2,440,000 in use just after World War II.

During these two decades when the boating industry enjoyed a boom which is not yet ended and for which the end does not seem in sight, the size of the boat and the size of the motor which powers it has edged constantly upward year by year. The average lengths of the outboard boats purchased in 1968, for instance, was almost 15½ feet, and the average horsepower of outboards sold that year was 31.5. The average horsepower of the outboards sold twenty years earlier, in 1948, by startling comparison, was only 5.2.

There is no doubt that boating has come into its own, whether it be as a one-day outing, a weekend cruise, or a month's-long adventure. Perhaps one reason is that our lakes, streams and oceans are places where the skyrocketing population of this nation can find elbow room. Three-fourths of this earth's surface is water and, once you get a mile or two away from the spot where you launch your family craft, you'll usually find room to breathe in solitude and peace. The area on both sides of the ramp or hoist may be a bustling and busy campground but, in most areas, only a few minutes' cruising time will take you to a remote beach where you can find the privacy which many of us long for.

Even a day or two of such privacy can do wonders in creating and maintaining unity. If you have more time available, this continent offers a vast number of boating pleasures. You can cruise the 247-mile-long protected waterway of the Trent-Severn canal in Canada's province of Ontario; the mighty Mississippi and the Missouri. Over 1,800 miles of shoreline, most of it deserted, awaits your exploration on Lake Powell out in Utah, mighty impoundment of the Colorado River formed by the new Glenn Canyon Dam. You can trailer your boat to Kino Bay on the mainland of Mexico, launch there and island-hop across the Gulf of California, never being more than 20 miles from a protecting bay, and make a landing on the 1000-mile-long peninsula of Baja California. From here you could turn southward and cruise the whole peninsula, ending up down at Cabo San Lucas. If you had the time, you could launch at Brownsville, Texas, take the Intra-Coastal Waterway around the Gulf of Mexico to Florida, then duck into the southern end of the St. Lawrence Waterway and cruise northward to Quebec City, bisecting the entire North American continent.

No, I'm not talking about buying a millionaire's ocean-going yacht. Plenty of boats are available today from 17 to 23 feet long, a size easily trailerable behind the family car, which will make such trips with comfort and safety. The technology of boatbuilding has advanced just as rapidly in the last decade as has any other form of human endeavor. The boats and marine engines offered by the boating industry to today's purchaser are incomparably superior to anything available in the 1950s.

Yes, family boating in today's vessels is a safe sport; probably the safest sport currently available. Official government records show that when the annual total of injuries and fatalities while boating are divided by the millions of boats in use this country, only a tiny fraction of 1 percent ever come to grief. A day on the water is far, far safer than the automobile drive you take to get to your craft, and boating is getting safer all the time. More rigid industry construction standards, improved marine facilities and increased boating education of the general public are all contributing to the reduction of even this minuscule percentage of tragedies.

There are two major marine trade organizations, the Boating Industry of America and the National Association of Engine and Boat Manufacturers. Most boat manufacturers belong to one or both. For them to be permitted to attach a BIA or an NAEBM plate to their product, it must meet stiff requirements that cover such widespread subjects as amount and location of flotation, ventilation systems for fuel compartments, bulk and displacement. This metal plate must state plainly how many passengers, or how many pounds of equipment, it can safely carry and also the maximum amount of horsepower the engine should be.

For several years now manufacturers have been taking this question of safety quite seriously, especially since boats made of fiberglass have practically crowded wood off of the market except for the largest of yachts. Since fiberglass won't float when swamped as a wood hull does, makers must build artificial flotation into their hulls. This is usually done by using a closed-cell material call styrofoam, either in solid blocks strapped and glassed into place, or by mixing the material and pouring it into the appropriate cavities in a liquid state. It then sets up and bonds itself to the hull. This is known as the foamed-in-place technique.

Just recently, the BIA stiffened its requirements to say that now a boat must not only float when completely swamped, but it must also float upright and not turn turtle. Some manufacturers even went further than this. As an example, one of the nation's largest builders of fiberglass boats launches and floods a sample of every new model before it goes into production. The boat must

Boating has become one of the most popular family sports in the nation, reflecting the need of people in overcrowded cities to seek privacy and quiet on lakes and streams. Increased boat size and outboard horsepower mean greater family participation in a variety of water sports.

stay upright or the design is discarded and the flotation system is rearranged. Then, when the boat successfully passes its final test and goes into production, individual specimens are pulled off at random and spotchecked in the same manner, by actual swamping.

If the safety factor of today's small boats is vastly improved, so too is the convenience of their layout. In great favor today is the open bow cockpit with windshield and steering position aft of it. This not only adds to the seating capacity but it's a great place for the youngsters to ride, up in front of Dad where he can keep an eye on them while also watching boating traffic.

Today's modern 17- or 28-footer is often a real sleep-aboarder. Lay-down lounge seats have been developed which provide back-to-back seating for four during the day, fold down into a pair of comfortable, full-length upholstered bunks at night. With a folding canvas top and a zipper-in fly covering the rest of the cockpit, she provides snug dry sleeping for two even on an extended camping or cruising trip. If the children are too big to sleep between Mom and Dad on air mattresses on the cockpit floor, a tent pitched ashore and some folding cots will take care of them nicely.

The same great strides have been made in marine engines; inboard, outboard and stern-drive. Whichever your choice, you will get performance, economy, power and reliability unknown even as little as ten years ago.

While being improved, safe boat handling has also been simplified. No more fooling around with spark advance and choke control levers and yanking on a rope; no more gear shifting and hoping you can do it without stripping gears or bending a shifting fork; no more steering with a tiller in an uncomfortably cramped and sidewise sitting position. Today you sit up forward in a comfortable club chair. In modern runabouts you have a steering wheel that works just like the family car's. You turn a key to start the engine. Most engines have just one control lever and shift from forward to reverse or into neutral automatically. You shove the lever ahead to go forward, pull it back to reverse and when it sticks straight up you are in neutral.

While the mechanical operation of a modern boat is simplicity itself, there are other skills you will need and these are easily available. Two excellent organizations, the United States Power Squadrons and the U.S. Coast Guard Auxiliary, offer free courses in seamanship and small-boat handling. There is hardly a community in this country so small that somewhere nearby one or the other organization will not be represented and offering these classes.

As you attend these sessions and learn basic seamanship and small-boat handling you will also discover both of them are fun organizations. You will make friends among your fellow boaters, both students and instructors, and will probably wind up joining the group, maybe eventually teaching a class yourself. They have good times at their meetings and social functions, usually stage a number of cruises each year, and are well worth belonging to. Initiation fee and dues are always nominal; only a few dollars a year.

So far we have only talked about family boating in engine-driven vessels. I admit that primarily my personal interest is in powerboats because I am at heart a fisherman, water skier and cruiser. It could well be, however, that a canvas-powered vessel will appeal to you more.

SAILBOATS

They don't use canvas for sails any more, of course; most of them are made of Dacron, except for the heavy-duty sails of long-distance, ocean-crossing vessels. Even then, if they are ocean-racing boats, they will use Dacron sails during the race and then switch to canvas for the trip home.

Sailboats are almost always considerably less expensive than power boats, foot for foot of length and capacity for capacity, both in initial purchase price and in operation. The wind is free, of course, and if the boat has an auxiliary engine its fuel demands are modest. With some companies, liability insurance premiums are lower. You can't go as fast as you can in a powerboat but you can have an awful lot of fun while getting there. Above all, there is a peace and quiet and a soothing quality of the water lapping against the hull as you slip silently through the waves.

If you do decide to go canvas rather than power, you might choose to purchase a combination racing and cruising vessel; one in which there is active competition. Then you could join your local yacht club and enjoy one of the most exciting family aquatic sports, yacht racing.

No, yacht racing and club membership do not require that you be a millionaire; at least, not the kind I'm talking about. There are many kinds of yacht racing to be enjoyed. Small fiberglass sailing boats, called "class boats," can be purchased complete with sails for as little as $1,000. They compete against other identical boats in match races and regattas. Some of these various classes are named Thistles, Lido 14s, Kites and Satellites; and there are others. Choose one which is popular in your neighborhood so that you know you'll have plenty of other boats against which to compete. Chrysler Marine Corporation has brought out a number of new racing yachts in the 16- to 18-foot length which are gaining in popularity, and strong competition in these classes is developing.

To race you must belong to an organized yacht club. However, this doesn't mean you have to spend thousands of dollars to join the fanciest club. What you can join is a "paper" yacht club; a legally organized group which has officers and bylaws, but which exists only on paper. It has no expensive clubhouse to maintain; all it does is hold regular meetings, usually dinner meetings in the banquet room of some restaurant, and exist to sponsor races. Dues in such clubs are often only ten or fifteen dollars a year, sometimes less, and the initiation fee is almost always twenty-five dollars or less. This includes an inspection of your boat by the Fleet Measurement Officer to make sure it is eligible to compete.

Anyone with a moderate income can get involved in yacht racing. Incidentally, the term yacht is quite properly applied to such vessels, as it is also to small power boats. According to the dictionary, a yacht is simply "a pleasure boat." There really are only three kinds of boats: commercial, men o' war and pleasure craft, and all used exclusively for pleasure are yachts while their owner is a yachtsman.

As much fun as sailing is, whether it be cruising or racing or a combination of both, it is still power-driven vessels which compose the bulk of the sales

Sailing retains its appeal for many people who enjoy the tranquility of slipping through the water in a wind-driven craft, or the excitement of racing against other members of a local yacht club.

each year and it is power that evokes the most public interest. Sales of such boats are booming and the interest is so strong that manufacturers of other types of sporting goods and camping accessories are tailoring their product to meet the demands of the families who want to go boat camping.

BOAT CAMPING

Gone are the days when a tent had to be a bulky affair weighing many pounds, cut from heavy canvas and with a system of wooden poles and guys that would have taxed a telephone company linesman to erect. Today you can get a tent just as large, just as sturdy, but cut from a light and strong poplin that weighs only a few pounds. Its frame will be made of aluminum which you can snap together in seconds.

No more heavy folding Army cots with oak frames. Instead you can buy one made of bent aluminum tubing that folds open or shut in seconds. It will have a wire-and-coil-spring webbing in the frame and a two-inch-thick foam mattress; will be far more comfortable than the old fashioned oak-and-canvas affair, yet will weigh only a pound or two, fold into a slim package—and costs about half as much as "Army cots."

All of the family camping gear has undergone this space-age modernization. Today's camp stove is almost as easy to cook on and regulate the flame as your regular gas stove at home. Lanterns perform equally well and are smaller and lighter than the old models. Pots, pans and dishes nest inside each other and the whole family's eating gear stows away in one small, lightweight package. Sleeping bags filled with modern synthetic fibers are twice as warm and half the weight of those we bought years ago.

One reason for this trend is that you do have to watch the weight and bulk of what you take along on your family outing. A modern planing hull is similar to an airplane in that there are just so many pounds it can lift. Overloaded, the boat will not only be unable to reach a planing speed but will also be loggy and unmanageable. That's why the BIA insists on that plate which tells you how many pounds or people it can safely carry. Weigh each carton of gear on the family bathroom scale before you place it aboard, keep a running total, allow for your fuel at the rate of 7 pounds per gallon and make sure the total is about 10 or 15 percent lower than the rated capacity of your boat. That way you'll have a margin to allow for anything you might add along the way.

You will also find that your food supply will have to take on a new look. If you will do your cruising on a water supply that is potable (and it is hardly a secret that there are fewer and fewer such waterways every year) you will be able to use modern concentrated and dehydrated foods that can be reconstituted before cooking and serving. However, if you are making a saltwater run or cruising some of our polluted inland waterways, you'll have to carry a supply of drinking water aboard and you won't want to use a precious drop of it for reconstitution. In this event you'd be better off to stock up on canned prunes rather than dried; fresh eggs rather than dehydrated.

The types of waterways to be cruised by small-boat skippers varies so greatly that no specific recommendations can be made here as to how to stock the galley. The important point is to research your cruising grounds thoroughly before leaving home. Among other things, you must determine your compass courses, landmarks, probable water depth, reefs, shoals and dangerous areas to be avoided. You'll want to know the prevailing direction of the wind and what the compass course is to the nearest harbor of refuge if it shifts. You'll want to know about the availability of fuel and how often and where you can restock the galley food supply.

You gather this information in a number of ways, and a great way to spend a long winter evening is planning next summer's family cruise. First, buy a copy of the book called the *United States Coast Pilot* which is appropriate to the area you intend to cruise. It's published by the United States Coast and Geodetic Survey. Many marine stores stock the various volumes, and you can order them by mail from Geodetic Survey, Washington, D.C.

This book describes in detail the various landmarks along shore and the character of the water on every navigable waterway in our whole nation. It tells you what the bottom is like, where to anchor and what to watch out for. Just get the volume which covers your proposed cruising area.

Boat camping is an ideal way to get away from crowded campgrounds and find sport and relaxation for the entire family. Lightweight camping equipment now available—tents, sleeping bags, cooking gear—won't overload a boat.

Next you should have a set of charts, also published by the U.S. Coast and Geodetic Survey, upon which to plot your trip. The book will tell you what numbers to order. By this time your navigational course with either the Power Squadron or the Coast Guard Auxiliary will have taught you how to plot a course, how to read a compass, the difference between magnetic and true north, how to swing ship and make a compass deviation card, how to compute the annual compass variation and how to run a rhumb line. Put all these newly acquired skills to work and by spring outfitting time you know where you are going, what to expect and what to avoid.

Two other good sources of information are the various major oil companies and local Chambers of Commerce. Almost any city of any size has its own C of C and a note addressed simply to "Chamber of Commerce" in any city along your route will usually bring a flood of brochures, resort information and maps about their area.

The big oil companies discovered some years ago that boats burn a lot of gasoline and ever since then they have wooed this class of trade most assiduously. A note to the head office of any of them asking for cruising information will bring you booklets, maps, information about local conditions and a list of their marine stations in any area you are interested in. In addition, most of them have prepared complete cruising manuals that are a mine of information.

So start gathering your gear together, acquiring your family boat-cruising kit and learning how to navigate your craft. As soon as the boating season starts in your area, make a few weekend trips as shakedown cruises in order to find out what is best for you and your family and what doesn't work out so well. Write for information, get your charts and your Coast Pilot and plan your adventurous journey. Then, when your summer vacation weeks roll around, you'll be ready to take off on the aquatic adventure of a lifetime. Or, if it's your family's pleasure, forsake the long cruise and the big boats. Make do with what you have—or rent. Either way, a world of pleasure awaits the sportsman and his family on lakes and streams.

6 A Walk in the Woods

ONE OF MY earliest and most vivid memories of an outdoor experience was the result of a hike one crisp winter morning immediately after a fresh snowfall. I was quite young and snow was relatively rare in our part of the country, and I still remember the awe with which I viewed the blanket of white from my bedroom window when my Dad gently shook me awake early that morning.

While the rest of the household slept we ate a quick breakfast, struggled into boots and heavy clothing, and stepped into the great white out-of-doors. It wasn't much of a hike, in reality, just a short walk into the woods surrounding our home. It wasn't much of a snowfall, if the truth be known, probably not more than three or four inches deep.

But the snowstorm had come and gone during the night, beginning after I went to bed and ending while the nocturnal creatures of the forest were still active. The gleaming blanket of white, therefore, contained a graphic record of the creatures which had passed that way since the snowfall ended. It was this record which Dad wanted me to see.

Not far from the house we came across the unmistakable imprint of a rabbit track. Dad explained to me that the two big marks of the rabbit track in the snow—the marks in front—were actually made by the hind feet of the rabbit, and that the two smaller ones—the ones farthest behind—were made by the front feet. I can still remember him demonstrating in the snow, when his explanation still left me puzzled as to just how the rabbit accomplished this startling thing.

We followed that rabbit track for quite a distance as it twisted, wound and retraced its steps, never straying very far from the spot where we first found it. Then, pointing out that the track had suddenly straightened out and that the distance between the tracks had become longer, Dad said, "Mr. Bunny is headed for his bed; we'll find him soon."

The outdoors contains many wonders for a youngster and his dog—a shoreline to explore, a tree to climb, an anthill in a field to puzzle over.

And it was't very long after that before we did find where the rabbit had made his bed. He had burrowed into a snowdrift beneath the base of a shrub and was almost buried. We approached very closely, and from a distance of only a few feet could peer down into the small hole and see one shining eye. I doubt that I will ever forget the spray of snow which resulted when we finally flushed the rabbit and watched him dash into the cover of the forest.

It is from such simple things that memories are made, and fathers and sons drawn nearer together.

Walk along an ocean beach to find driftwood, bottles, fishnet floats, sand crabs, shells and other objects to stir the curiosity of young and old.

In the years that followed Dad guided me, with love, patience and understanding, to an appreciation of nature. He taught me to value all of the aspects of the outdoors—the *sight* of a spider web shining in the early-morning sun, sparkling with dew; the *sound* of a bobwhite's clear ringing whistle echoing across the cornfield; the *smell* of a honeysuckle in bloom; the *feel* of a fresh breeze upon my brow, signifying the approach of a summer storm. These things and a thousand more do I cherish about the outdoors, and an appreciation of them has made more meaningful my outings in the field, whether they have been for fishing, for hunting, for camping, for boating, or for any other pursuit of the sportsman.

It is an appreciation of values such as these that I have tried to pass on to my wife and to my children. A conscious effort to do so is required, for we "veteran" outdoorsmen too frequently take for granted the simple yet vital bits of knowledge we have acquired. In making the effort to pass on these things to your family, you'll find that your own life is enriched.

In the twenty-five years since Mary and I were married, some of the most fruitful and enjoyable hours, days and weeks have been those I spent giving to her and to the children the bits of information about the outdoors which seemed appropriate at the time. Not so surprisingly, it frequently turned out that I ended up getting the greatest education of all, for it is amazing the questions wives and youngsters can ask about even the simplest things.

Nature can be harsh, and sometimes dangerous, but even the poisonous cottonmouth moccasin prefers to be left alone.

Some of the walks in the woods we have enjoyed during the past years have been in remote wilderness areas of the nation, but most of them have been in much more ordinary places—such as our backyard. Or in the city park. Or along the shores of the city reservoir.

Enjoy the bits and pieces of nature to the fullest when you come across them. A casual study of nature, after all, is what our walks are. Opportunities for this are endless no matter who you are or where you live. All it takes is just an awareness and willingness to ask: What is it? Why is it? How is it? And then to seek the answers if you don't know them.

Try taking your youngster into the backyard sometime and digging for him a fishing worm. Explain to him how earthworms operate. Show him that they have no eyes, that none are necessary because they live in a lightless environment underground. Explain that earthworms feed by passing a quantity of the soil through their bodies, and that collectively the worms are responsible for aerating and tilling tons of earth.

Toss that worm out on the lawn and it's likely that a bird will fly down to snatch it up before very long. That gives you an opportunity to tell your child that earthworms are one of the major items in the diet of robins, and that when robins cock their heads to one side when hopping around on the lawn, they aren't *looking* for worms; they are actually *listening* for worms. Eye-

Tracks reveal the habits of the unseen creatures of the outdoors. A deer in a hurry and a leisurely raccoon left their marks on this sandbar.

sight? Yes, birds have exceptionally good eyesight, and the birds of prey—hawks and eagles—have the best eyesight of all. From an altitude of hundreds of feet they can spot a small rodent in the grass, and it is believed that their eyesight is comparable to that of a man using a pair of eight-power binoculars.

And isn't it a shame about the birds of prey, particularly the beautiful peregrine falcon. Like the pelicans we shall talk about in the chapter on bird watching, only more so, the falcons are at the head of the food chain, and in such position they have been receiving massive doses of pesticides such as DDT.

How do they get the DDT? Well, DDT is applied to the landscape and gets into the soil. There, the earthworm which passes that soil through his body, ends up with a small amount of the DDT left in it. Along comes the robin and eats the worm, and another worm, and another worm, and stores up in its body all of this accumulation of poison. When the falcon makes its screaming dive into a flock of robins, the bird that it catches is the slowest one, the one which has been weakened by the heaviest concentration of DDT.

As is the case with the pelicans, when the level of DDT reaches a certain concentration in falcons the females lay eggs with shells which are too thin to withstand incubation. The incubating parent breaks the eggs accidentally,

A cougar passed this way . . .

. . . and a grizzly left his unmistakable print in the snow.

and no young result from the nesting that year. In this fashion the peregrine falcon has been virtually eliminated from the eastern half of the United States, and the population greatly reduced through the nation.

See how the chain grows! From that simple earthworm you have been led to think and talk of soil tillage and robins and bird eyesight and falcons and DDT. Each time you venture into an investigation of any facet of nature with your youngsters, you can expect just such ramifications.

What fun it is to see nature through the eyes of children. Mary and I simply had a wonderful time helping Barbara, Tom and Kent investigate the new world of the ocean shore on their first visit to the coast. What makes the ocean get higher and then lower? Why doesn't the ocean ever get still and calm like our lake? What made that old tree on the beach so smooth? What kind of seashell is that?

Sand, wind, tracks, tide, waves, seagulls, bottles, driftwood, sandcrabs, sandfleas, jellyfish, ocean breeze, rocks, sand dunes, sand pipers, shadows, periwinkles.

As an outgrowth of her love of history, Mary is an antique collector. The antiques may or may not have monetary value, but they represent an era of our history which has passed, and as such are keys to understanding what made our country. Bottle collecting is one of her favorites, and it has also become one of the favorite outdoor activities of the rest of the family.

Much of our beachcombing has been done with a keen eye for old bottles, and we have dug countless holes in the sand seeking a treasure. Most of those holes have been dry ones, but occasionally the rewards are great.

These old bottles have been a vehicle through which we have taught history to our youngsters. Each one of them represents a specific period in the life of our country, and it is an interesting challenge to try to run down the origin of each of the fragile relics we find. When children can actually pick up and feel a flask thrown aside two centuries ago by some British Redcoat officer, as ours did when Mary discovered two such bottles on an island off the coast of South Carolina, that particular bit of history is more than a few dull lines in a book.

We live on a lake. I almost said that we are fortunate to live on a lake, and we are, but it goes a bit deeper than that. Mary and I planned it this way, and any sacrifices we may have made along our route to this point are more than justified by the watery wonderland at our doorstep.

From our back patio we watch egrets and herons stand quietly along our shoreline, now and then making a rapier-like thrust into the water to spear a squirming fish. We watch the swirl of water as the male bluegill drives an intruder away from his spawning bed. We listen to the melodious sound of the bullfrog and see the track of the mink in the soft mud along the shore.

It's easier for my family to enjoy these aquatic pleasures now that we do live on a lake, but it is possible for almost any sportsman and his family to do the same with only a little more effort. We did it before we became lakeside dwellers. There are few places in this nation which are more than a few minutes, distance from some kind of a pond or stream.

When you are outdoors with your young children, occasionally drop down to their level and get a new perspective. Things look different from a location two or three feet off the ground than they do from your six-foot elevation. The small living things, plant and animal, are much more apparent when you are down close to them—insects, bees, seeds, flowers.

The wonders of camouflage are ever-present sources of amazement and enjoyment to those who will look. A chameleon, a praying mantis, a woodcock, a copperhead on a background of fall leaves, gull eggs on a shell-strewn beach. Each is a capsule lesson in conservation.

A walk in the woods with your family, whether it be a five-minute backyard stroll or a more ambitious expedition, is a simple outdoor activity which is fun for all. It is also a perfect opportunity to instill into your youngsters a love and appreciation of all nature.

7 Bird Watching

IF YOU ARE a sportsman, you are a bird watcher. Perhaps you've never thought of yourself as such, but during your travels in the outdoors, hunting, fishing and boating, you've been a bird watcher all along. Even casually, unknowingly, you've marked the passage of a flight of ducks, a flock of geese, or the cry of a loon or a woodthrush at twilight. You're a casual member of a vast and ever-growing army of people who intensely enjoy the hobby of bird watching.

Bird watching can be an exciting and pleasurable activity for your wife and your children when they join you in the outdoors. They can participate in this activity as casually as most sportsmen, as intently as most dedicated bird watchers, or to any degree in between.

Bird watching, like most outdoor activities, is fun, but as your family's guide you can stress the educational value in this particular outdoor hobby. And in addition to the pleasure and the education bird watchers derive from their hobby, in many cases they contribute directly to the cause of conservation.

It is the perfect family sport, which may be pursued in your neighborhood park, your own backyard or in a remote wilderness. Virtually everywhere on earth, except for the South Pole, there are birds to be observed and studied. This hobby is one that makes you dig for knowledge. You may soon find your family visiting the library to identify that odd little fellow you saw on your last trip. You will also discover it is a very healthful pastime when you begin making field trips. It's a little like a golfer who would never go for a three or four mile walk if he weren't knocking a little ball ahead of him. You'll cover a lot of miles and enjoy every minute of it.

Watching and studying birds goes back to the earliest history of man. Hunger probably spurred his interest. The eggs of all birds are good to eat when freshly laid and the flesh of most of them is delicious. In San Francisco in the 1850s, for instance, chicken's eggs were unknown. Smart promoters acquired boats, made the cruise over to the Farralon Islands offshore, robbed the nests in the

107

seagull rookery there and sold them in the markets of that cosmopolitan city at exorbitant prices. It was customary for chefs to crack these eggs in the outdoors because no one could guarantee how long they might have lain in the nest before being gathered.

The oldest known bird, brought down to us only in fossil form, inhabited Bavaria. Found in the Solnhofen limestone deposits of that country, it has

Many bird watchers take up photography in order to record observed species. The sportsman gets many chances for bird photos on hunting and fishing jaunts. The author caught this owl during a squirrel hunt.

been named *Archaeopteryx lithographica*. Translated from the Latin, it means "ancient winged creature of the stone for drawing." It is of great interest because it forms a link between the reptiles from which modern birds originated and today's winged flyers. It had a long tail with twenty vertebrae, three fingers with claws on each hand, an uncomplicated backbone with no fusions of the vertebrae, simple ribs, no fusions of the handbones and a simple brain. The wings, however, resembled those of modern birds. So too did some of the bones in the hips. Another similarity to modern birds was the collarbone, which joins to form a wishbone. This type of skeletal formation is found in birds alone among animals. It was probably a horrible looking thing. Its flight must have been limited because its bones were solid, not hollow, so it was probably only capable of gliding from tree branch to tree branch. Its feathers evolved as an adaptation to increase its arm area, grip the air and steady it in its long, gliding leaps.

So man has always been fascinated by the feathered creatures on this planet. As long ago as the 1500s the first organized study group was formed: the Academy of the Secrets of Nature, in Naples. It researched all of the field of natural history. The first group dedicated solely to the study of birds was formed in 1851: the German Ornithological Society. The first such group in this country was the Nuttall Ornithological Club, founded in 1873, which is still going strong today.

The Audubon Society, however, is the organization which most people think of as being composed of bird watchers. In reality, the Audubon Society is interested in all forms of nature. Of particular interest to the sportsman and his family are chapters of the Audubon Society in most sizable cities throughout the United States. Attending a few meetings of the chapter nearest your home, and participating in a few of their field trips, may be an excellent way to interest your family in this hobby. Joining with other bird watchers in groups such as this may be the natural outgrowth of your having introduced your family to the hobby during your normal outdoor outings.

BIRD WATCHING AND CONSERVATION

Bird watching is a natural, easy way of teaching young people about the mistreatment of our environment. In just the past two centuries, for instance, seventy-six species of birds have disappeared, have become totally extinct. More than half of them have disappeared because of man's activities. Humans, intent on polluting their world, on poisoning its air, water and soil, have raped the planet which is their home. Wildlife suffers as does man, and chief among the sufferers is the bird population.

Using bird watching as a vehicle, you can teach your youngsters that the greatest threat to bird life existing today is the pesticides known as the chlorinated hydrocarbons. The most common of these are DDT, Dieldrin and Aldrin, and it is significant that the U.S. Department of Interior has recommended that the use of DDT be ended completely.

An example of the detrimental effect of DDT is found in a study currently being made concerning those majestic flyers, the pelicans. In the spring of 1969, not one single live chick was found in the nests in the pelican rookery located in the Channel Islands off the California coast. All—and this means hundreds of thousands—of the eggs were smashed in the nests. Why?

Explain to your children that the pelican is at the head of a food chain which funnels food items bearing an ever greater concentration of pesticide to the big birds. DDT has two properties which make it particularly dangerous: it is extremely long-lived, more than ten years; it accumulates in the bodies of the creatures which ingest it in nonlethal amounts.

DDT applied to the land eventually makes its way to the sea, and there into the minute organisms of the ocean. The food chain which begins there ends, in our case, with the pelican, which receives the accumulation of DDT which has been stored by all the creatures in between.

When the concentration of DDT in the pelican reaches a certain amount, the effect is simple and deadly. It causes the females to produce eggs which have shells that are extremely thin, so thin that incubation causes them to break before they have an opportunity to hatch.

There is, I repeat, not one single live pelican chick on any of the Pacific Coast Channel Islands. Meanwhile, state and federal authorities continue to argue about whether the situation is as serious as people say it is.

There are groups and societies vitally interested in bird conservation, organizations that do what they can to protect endangered species. The first of them was started in Pennsylvania in 1886. A brilliant naturalist, George Bird Grinnell, named it after John James Audubon, the artist whose paintings of birds of both Europe and America are still highly valued by naturalists.

The Audubon Society is still prominent in the field of conservation, and has done a great deal toward keeping the destruction of our wildlife to its present level. Other organizations, such as the Wildlife Management Institute, Ducks Unlimited, the Isaac Walton League and the National Wildlife Federation, plus a huge number of concerned individuals who belong to no organized group, have led the battle toward public awareness of the dangers facing wildlife.

GETTING STARTED

The best-known bird identification guides are Peterson's field guides, Chapman's handbook and the Golden field guide. All sportsmen should have at least one of these. It would also be a good idea to drop a note to the director of the department of fish and game in your capitol, and ask him to send you all the booklets he has that pertain to birds in your state. Most departments have quite a few valuable publications, well illustrated, and usually they are free for the asking.

Let me make it clear that there are right and wrong ways to introduce your family to the hobby of bird watching. I can imagine Mary's reaction, a couple of decades ago, if I had stated, "This week, Mary, we are going to take up bird watching." I am sure her reaction would have been, "Are you crazy?"

Her actual introduction to bird watching began when I first started her dove hunting, and my problem was to teach her the difference between a dove and a meadowlark. I was not always entirely successful, much to the sorrow of the meadowlarks.

Other bird identification came as a matter of course. She learned the soaring hawks and buzzards which were most conspicuous in the sky, the quail we hunted, the roadrunners, the swallows and the killdeers, which also so closely resemble doves. Her education in water birds progressed in like fashion, when she started to go with me on fishing trips. Egrets, herons, kingfishers, cormorants—all became part of her vocabulary. Observation taught her, and she soon learned that the fish were where the birds were.

We introduced our children to bird watching in much the same fashion, although I must confess that it was with an ulterior motive at times. When traveling between camping sites, for instance, it was helpful to have something to keep the youngsters occupied in the car. Spotting and identifying birds along the road was an excellent distraction.

We made a game of seeing which one of the children could spot the birds quickest along the roadside, on telephone lines, or in the air, and which could identify them first. They got extra points if they knew which ones were migratory and which were non-migratory, which were game birds and which were non-game birds. As knowledge increased, we added value for additional information about the bird itself: nesting habits, number of young, range, identifying characteristics. As their knowledge grew, so did their interest.

Bird watching, as is readily seen by these examples, can be extremely simple. The only equipment we needed was a guidebook in the glove compartment to settle the arguments; and there were arguments, as I rapidly found out when I began trying to identify for my youngsters the numerous species of birds encountered in our travels.

EXPANDING YOUR KNOWLEDGE

Now that you have your family interested, it's probable that your next step will be a bit of study. First, you might list the names of the birds that can reasonably be expected to be seen in your area. Then, learn how to identify them. Some birds can be identified by color alone, as the roseate spoonbill of the southeastern swamps or the big bluejays found almost everywhere. Mostly, however, identification is accomplished by the presence of spots or stripes in the coloring, rings of color on breast, wings, tail and eyes. Intensity of color should also be recorded: vibrant, pale, iridescent or drab.

You should learn accepted common names of these birds, and perhaps later on even their scientific names.

Now, you see, your family has not only acquired a new hobby; it's possible they have also become researchers who will add to man's knowledge of his environment. Like most bird clubs, they may conduct scientific studies, make records, record patterns of behavior and study the interrelationship of common and rare species and the effect they have on each other. They will learn that birdlife is changing every minute just as is man himself. Some species can adapt to change; some cannot and fall by the wayside.

The famous condor, mighty buzzard of the West, failed to do so, and this huge bird with an 8-foot wingspread is now down to just forty known specimens. Living and breeding on a mountain called Condor Peak in Angeles National Forest near Los Angeles, the bird is very timid. Almost any unusual sight or sound, particularly the presence of man, will cause the hen to abandon her nest. Since she only lays and hatches one egg every two years, the encroachment of civilization has all but wiped out the species. Even an airplane flying high overhead will frighten her off of her nest, leaving the incubating egg to die. Airlines try to route their flights away from Condor Peak but private planes sometimes buzz the area and the damage is done.

On the other hand there is the dove, both the whitewing and the mourning dove. Both of these species have adapted to civilization and are prospering. There are far more doves in this country today than there were when the continent was a primitive wilderness. Some estimates say there are a hundred times as many doves living and prospering. During the hunting season each fall, many millions are harvested with no adverse effect on the resource. One state alone, California, takes over four *million* birds each year and yet the species continues to prosper.

One activity which bird-watching families can participate in is the annual census conducted by the Audubon Society. Every year along about Christmas time, all of the local chapters take to the field, notebooks in hand, and record on the Society's standard form what they see and where. This data, collected and correlated against information gathered in previous years, forms a most important file of information on what is happening to America's bird population.

Changes are certainly taking place. Even birds are affected by alterations in environment made by man. They change their social customs accordingly. One family which lives on the waterfront has discovered the fun of bird watching by conducting a continuing study of the habits of a flock of wild mallards that lives on the bay right outside their front door. Some of their findings are interesting.

For one thing, this flight of about fifty wild mallards never migrates; winter and summer, they call the bay home. Personality traits of individual birds vary widely—some are aggressive, some are sullen, some are friendly and some are cry babies, always being picked on by the others and squawking over it.

Two pairs have become housepets even though originally they were wild, migrating waterfowl. This family buys corn for the flock and feeds the whole band of them daily. However, if they are late with the feeding, these two pairs will flop up on the dock, waddle across the patio and peck on the door to remind the family that it is feeding time. These four ducks eat from the hand and have been taught table manners—they each wait for their turn to be fed and never try to grab grain from a handful intended for another of the four.

Even here, in this controlled environment, changes are taking place. In the last couple of years, a few domestic white Pekins are appearing—ordinary ranch ducks raised for eating. Presumably, as day-old ducklings they were given to children in the neighborhood as Easter presents, and later released in the bay.

Now the Pekins have mated with mallards, and the breeding habits of the latter have changed. The males no longer perform the breeding dance to seduce the females, the classical routine which must be performed by the wild mallard male before the female becomes aroused and accepts his advances. The new generation of crossbred ducks simply breeds by force, with no mating dance and parade at all. In the flock of ducklings produced by such unions, there is no intermingling of physical characteristics; part of the eggs will hatch out as pure, all-white Pekins; others will be pure greenhead mallards showing nothing of their white-feathered parents' appearance. Sometimes they go all one way or the other. This year one white Pekin female successfully raised to adulthood fifteen ducklings, every one of them with purely mallard markings. Not a trace of the mother showed in them, although they followed her around the bay all spring.

Such interesting studies as these are constantly being made by independent observers, people who may have started their bird-watching activity by playing games with their children while traveling between campsites.

You and your family can have a great deal of pleasure observing birds at home, if you live anywhere except in a city apartment building. Feeders can be constructed, bird baths set in the garden, wild birdseed scattered at a certain time every day. You'll be surprised how many birds will put you on their social visiting list.

A sure device for luring birds, especially in the wintertime, is a suet feeder. Get a small piece of hardware cloth, cut it with tinsnips and fold it to make a box about 6 inches long, 3 inches wide and about an inch thick. Into this stuff pieces of raw beef tallow, trimmed from the family's steaks, chops and roasts. Tie it securely to a tree limb, a fence post, or anywhere off the ground in a location where you can get an unobstructed view of it. In no time at all the birds will discover it is there and begin to peck at and eat chunks of the tallow. During cold weather, particularly, they like this fat and it's good for them.

Hummingbird feeders are a lot of fun, and there is hardly a portion of our country where hummingbirds aren't found. These are the only birds in the world which can hover in midair and even fly backward. You can buy a feeder at most pet shops and bird stores. It is a little glass vial with a slender, hollow tube coming out of one side. Fill it with a sugar syrup and hang it in a tree or outside the window. The hummingbird will hover in midair in front of it, stick his long delicate beak down into the tube and eat his fill. You will find that the same birds visit you at almost the same time every day.

Wild birdseed can be purchased at many pet shops, feed stores and even some supermarkets, but don't overdo the feeding. It is best to scatter just enough grain to attract the birds, but not enough to make it become a regular feeding process.

Explain to your family that it simply isn't good for them. If you put out enough grain to really sustain them, the birds turn into bums. They quit working for a living, get fat and soon succumb to disease. Like human beings on the dole, they tend to become panhandlers. Moderate feeding of the purchased grain will not hurt them and will get them in the habit of using your feeding station.

OPTICAL EQUIPMENT

Although you can start your family bird watching with no elaborate equipment, it probably won't be long before you find they will want optical equipment for better viewing. This means a pair of binoculars or a telescope, and a great many of you sportsmen will already own either one or both.

Binoculars are almost a must for even semiserious bird watching. Even at close range they are needed to pick out the identifying characteristics which separate different species of sparrows or warblers, for instance, and at long range to tell a flock of baldpates from a flock of gadwalls. They can be quickly brought to bear on the object of your attention and they can be used for hours without strain.

There was a time when the only good binoculars were expensive binoculars, and some of my favorites are still quite costly. Among these are the excellent Bausch and Lomb glasses manufactured in this country, with the 7 x 35 Zephyr-Light glass being one of the favorites among birders. The latter sells for about $200. Another superb binocular is the Leitz Trinovid, which features a unique prism design which permits a substantial reduction in the size of the glass. My 10 x 40 Trinovids, for instance, measure only 5½ by 4¾ by 1¾ inches, weigh only 22 ounces. They cost slightly less than $300, which is expensive when the initial price of the glass is considered, but nominal if that price is prorated over the long life of the instrument. Such glasses as the Bausch and Lomb and the Trinovids will last for years and years if properly cared for.

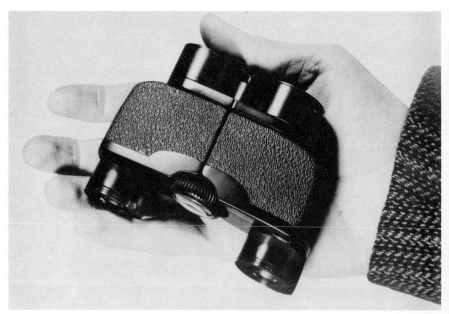

Bushnell Custom Compact binoculars, available in 6X and 7X, are lightweight, small and weatherproof—good glasses for children.

Insta-Focus feature of new Bushnell binoculars is an aid to bird watchers as it permits focusing through the entire range of the glass with a slight movement of the thumb.

There was also a time when the term "Made in Japan" denoted poor workmanship. That time has long since passed. This is particularly true in the field of optics, since some of the finest cameras in the world are produced in Japan.

This mushrooming Japanese optical industry has, since World War II, placed excellent binoculars within the reach of any sportsman. That is not to say that all of the optics coming into this country from Japan are good, but the reputable importers attempt to screen out all inferior products. One of these importers is D. P. Bushnell and Company, Bushnell Building, Pasadena, California 91107.

Dave Bushnell is a young Californian who has established his reputation by guaranteeing the quality of the Japanese optics which he imports. Establishing quality control in some of the Japanese factories was a difficult thing to do in the early days following World War II, but Dave persisted to the point where he can now offer a twenty-year guarantee on his best products. Even his best ones are relatively inexpensive.

We own several pairs of binoculars. The Bushnell Custom Compacts is the pair that my youngsters usually fight for when we head for the field. This superb little glass weighs only 11 ounces and will fit into your shirt pocket, yet it provides a crystal clear 6-power magnification. In the 6 power, it lists for $65, the 7 power for $70.

Bushnell has a line of regular-sized binoculars, including one which features a new development of interest to bird watchers which is called Insta-Focus. With a slight movement of the thumb, the binocular can be focused rapidly throughout the full focusing range, and this is quite an advantage to a bird watcher trying to focus quickly on a rare specimen. It also has its advantages, needless to say, for a big-game hunter attempting to evaluate the rack on a rapidly moving deer.

In these days of species management, of course, the duck hunter *must* be an avid bird watcher. In making sure that he shoots at the right legal species and refrains from shooting at those which are protected, a binocular is a great aid.

Another answer to better seeing is the monocular, which is half of a binocular. The advantage is that it is smaller and costs quite a bit less. The disadvantage is that it is not nearly so pleasant to use.

For those who don't use a spotting scope, a useful aid is the Binocular-Spotter, an attachment for Bushnell binoculars which increases the magnification 2½ times.

The next step up the line in optics, one used by many serious bird watchers, is the telescope. The occasions when the use of the telescope is called for are more limited than those permitting the use of binoculars, of course, but there are some when it is invaluable. My family has spent hours on a lake bank scoping a raft of ducks far offshore. With the high magnification of the telescope, steadily mounted on a tripod, we could not only determine the species of the individual birds in the flock, but in most instances determine male or female, juvenile or adult.

The same Bushnell Spacemaster telescope which I use for glassing antelope and sheep does double duty with my family when it comes to bird watching. Bausch and Lomb also makes an excellent telescope.

Bushnell also has an interesting monocular arrangement which snaps into one side of their binoculars to increase the magnification. It is called a Binocular Telescope Attachment, sells for $20, and increases the magnification from 7x to 17x. It is an excellent compromise for one who prefers the binocular and who does not want to carry the extra load of a telescope along. For the bird watcher it has the obvious advantage of being available for that extra power when that hard-to-identify specimen comes along.

OTHER EQUIPMENT

The total equipment for even the serious bird watcher, then, is quite simple. It consists of an identification field guide to the birds, and usually a pair of binoculars. One other rather insignificant, yet quite important, item is some form of a notebook. In this, the bird watcher keeps his lifetime "bird list," jotting down in it each of the species which he has personally identified. In this notebook you can record simply the species of the bird, or you can go into such detail as the date on which you identified it, the location and the circumstances.

A great many bird watchers eventually want to record their bird lists on film as well as in notebooks. This is a specialized form of outdoor photography dealt with in some length in the chapter following this one. While the photographing of some bird species can be extremely difficult, let me emphasize that satisfying results are within reach of almost everyone.

Photographing rare and hard to approach bird life is a challenging and most worthwhile adventure, but it is still true that the capturing on film of a robin at a backyard bird feeder is still satisfying fun for most families. That can be accomplished with a minimum amount of ingenuity and equipment by almost anyone.

Attracting birds by imitating their calls is one of the ways bird watchers get them near enough to identify. The individual can do this by using his own vocal cords, if he is skillful enough, or by using a mouth or hand call mechanically, or by replaying the recorded voices of these species. Many birds will come to a squeaking sound, and "bird squeakers" are available which mechanically produce such a squeak to attract birds. You can get the same squeaking results by sucking on the back of your hand.

WHERE TO GO

The bird watching and recording you do in your own yard will usually be over the feeding and watering stations you have set up. Locate them so that you have a good view from your windows, and close enough so that your binoculars and camera will give you a good-sized image.

For most of us, bird watching is a welcome fringe benefit of our other trips into the outdoors, not usually requiring a special junket for birding purposes. Whether we are fishing or hunting, camping or boating, hiking or traveling between campsites, the opportunities for observing our feathered friends are almost ever present.

When you are making a special effort to observe birds, of course, your objective should be to blend into the landscape and become an unobtrusive part of the scene. The same rules apply here as apply to the deer hunter on his stand, which is why a good deer hunter gets so many opportunities to observe bird life.

I find quite a similarity in the actions of the bird life which inhabits our backyard and the bird life which I find on pack trips into the remote wilderness areas of the nation. Those in my yard are so accustomed to human beings that they pay little attention to them, while those in the wilderness areas have seen so few people—if any—that they can be closely approached by the careful observer. The rule here is to move slowly and cautiously, never in such a manner as to constitute a threat to the birds you are trying to watch.

Our family does make some special trips primarily for bird watching and yours may find that desirable too. The national wildlife refuges and the national parks are among the finest areas in the nation for such observation. On the Aransas National Wildlife Refuge on the coast of Texas, for instance, wintertime visitors may be able to observe the whooping crane, one of the rarest of all the birds.

The city parks in the midst of our biggest cities are oases where bird life thrives, furnishing the city dweller with a nearby opportunity to enjoy this fine hobby. Fish hatchery ponds and city water-supply reservoirs are frequently treasure chests of opportunities for bird watchers where aquatic species are concerned.

Members of my family are bird watchers in both a casual and a semiserious way, depending upon the situation and the circumstance. We enjoy it both ways, and this interest has occupied many hours for Mary and the youngsters while I was engaged in the very serious pursuit of fin, fur and feather. Give it half a chance and odds are good that your family will enjoy it, too.

8   Outdoor Photography

HAVE YOU ever sat in a valley where a bubbling stream flowed over massive boulders, beautiful green pines grew thickly on the hillsides and in the distance towering snowcapped peaks climbed to the heavens? Perhaps you've walked along pebble-strewn beaches as the ocean crashed against the shore, where high sand dunes and twisted red-berried holly trees provided a picturesque setting.

Such scenes are commonplace in the outdoors. For years to come you'll recall their beauty, but with the passage of time many memories fade—unless you capture these scenes on film.

It is not just the spectacular scenes which the average sportsman and his family want to recall. For most of us, it is the everyday happenings which enhance any simple outing. Remember how Junior looked when he caught his first bluegill? How about the time Pop was trying to learn to water ski? Wouldn't it have made a great picture when Granddad was here a few years ago, and he charcoaled those hamburgers on a makeshift grill on the back lawn? Get the big impressive scenes on film, too, of course, but it's the little things that mean a lot as the years go by.

Photography can be fun for the entire family, because everyone sees different things in the outdoors. The sportsman may want to record a fine catch he made along a quiet beat of stream, while the sportsman's wife finds the land-scape breathtaking and the youngsters capture on film a mother robin and her hungry young. When everyone finds how exciting photography can be, and all contribute to composing fine pictures of their activities, the results are enjoyed by the entire family for years to come.

The great advances made in cameras, photography equipment and film in the last decade have contributed in great part to the growing popularity of picture taking in the outdoors. Where years ago cameras were complex tools, today the use of even fine-quality cameras may be mastered in just a couple of evenings of study. With simple cameras it simply becomes a matter of loading up and shooting pictures, usually with gratifying results—results, it should be noted, that would have been impossible even with expensive cameras a score of years ago.

Unfortunately, many a would-be camera enthusiast is stymied from the first moment he enters a camera store. It can be, and often is, a frightening experience for someone who doesn't know anything about photography. There are many different types of cameras, and dozens of brands of each type. There isn't just a single lens for many cameras, for a dozen or more lenses may be used with many of them! There are light meters, flashguns, flashbulbs, flash cubes and electronic flash. There are films galore and even more filters than there are films.

It isn't really as complicated as it may seem. Like most hobbies, you've got to go about photography systematically, starting with basic equipment and then, as you gain experience, expanding upon your equipment and the techniques you use to achieve fine-quality photographs.

If you are already a photographer, then you won't need the basic instructions in this chapter to pass on to your family. If you are not, keep in mind this thought: Don't overwhelm either yourself or your family in the beginning.

Most sportsmen will not want to delve deeply into outdoor photography at first, and perhaps never. Their interest lies in the primary outdoor activities of hunting, fishing, camping or boating, and getting pictures of these activities is only a pleasant and rewarding adjunct to them. It will probably be that way with your family, so keep it very simple when you are initiating them into this fine activity.

COMPOSITION

Perhaps the biggest secret of successful outdoor photography is composition. During the past few years there has been a tendency among many photographers simply to point their camera and to shoot, shoot, shoot. This is done on the theory that film is cheap and you're bound to get some good pictures if you shoot enough film. Granted, this approach will get an occasional good shot, but most of your shooting will be a waste of film, and you'll never have the pride that comes from carefully composing a picture and knowing that the beauty of the finished product is a result of your own forethought.

Composition is done on the groundglass of your camera or the viewfinder. When you look at the groundglass observe everything that is on it. Often when you view a particular scene your eyes have a habit of not seeing what you don't want to see. When you look across a valley at a mountain rising towards the sky your eyes sometimes overlook the unsightly high-tension wires that may cross a corner of the picture you plan to take. There may be some unsightly debris in the foreground, even though your eyes are focusing on the background. Likewise, if you're taking closeups, make certain you look behind your subject to ascertain that the background won't detract from the subject matter.

There are many ways in which unwanted items can be removed either from the foreground or background. Sometimes it's simply a matter of taking the picture from a different angle. Occasionally you may have to walk up a hill to get a better angle, or perhaps you may have to lie down to get a good shot. Occasionally you can use natural foliage to block out something you may not want to appear in the picture.

Don't be afraid to get unusual angles. So many people always shoot while standing up. Try kneeling down, or even lying on the ground. You'll be

Example of good composition is this photo of a western packtrain moving along a river bank. Diagonal line of bank and packtrain leads the eye toward the center, as do the diagonals formed by stand of pines and distant mountain.

pleasantly surprised at how different things look because of the different lens angle.

Another secret is occasionally to frame your picture, to put the scene in proper perspective. If you're out in the woods and want to shoot an animal grazing along the edge of the woods, you don't have to get to the edge and just have the animal in your picture. Stay just inside the wooded area and use the trunks of several trees to frame the game you are photographing. Even small shrubs can be used to good effect for framing.

Good camera angle and unobtrusive background contribute to this crisp portrait of Montana outfitter.

Framing the landscape with trees in the foreground gives depth to both photos on facing page, which otherwise would have been flat and uninteresting.

122

Do the same thing with fishing pictures. If someone in the family is wading a stream, photograph him from a high spot along the bank, shooting through the trees. It gives that feeling of being out in the wilderness, and certainly looks far prettier than an angler simply standing in the stream, completely surrounded by nothing but water. Even dockside pictures can be given impact by framing one side of the picture with a dock piling, or shooting through the ropes holding a boat snug against the wharf. Lobster pots can frame a picture, as can a rod or gun leaning against a tree. Don't overdo framing, however. It's nice on a few pictures, but like everything else, can lose its effectiveness through repetition.

Balance your photography by taking closeups, medium shots and long shots. Even with normal lenses you can easily do this. If you're fishing, get a closeup of a catch of fish *and* the rod, reel and lures that caught them; a normal shot of a person fighting or landing the fish, using the person's body to fill the frame so you have impact. Then get a mood shot from about 20 feet away of the person just fishing. Perhaps you can wind up the series with something in the background, such as a couple of trail horses drinking at the edge of the stream while the angler wades and is in crisp focus in the center of the picture

DEPTH-OF-FIELD

You can get good results through the wise use of depth-of-field. Depth-of-field is the area of your picture which is in sharp focus. The more you have to open your lens, the less picture area is in focus; the foreground and background tend to be out of focus, thus making your subject stand out. This is very noticeable in most advertising photography, where the product stands out crisply defined and everything else is fuzzy.

Depth-of-field isn't difficult to master. Just be conscious that it's always available and easy to use to good advantage. Shooting with a shutter speed of 1/60 second with a lens opening of f/22, focused at 15 feet, everything from 8 to 60 feet would be in sharp focus. But you can shoot at 1/500 second with the lens opened to f/8. This way you have sharp focus only between 12 and 20 feet, with the foreground and background out of focus.

On the other hand, you may want the greatest depth of field possible. If so, use the smallest lens opening, adjusting the shutter speed accordingly to the correct exposure.

ACTION PHOTOS

In outdoor photography there is often movement. Perhaps you're skiing, fishing or hunting. Where there is movement you have to anticipate this movement and attempt to release your shutter at the peak action. This may be when a fish is jumping, or a skier making a turn with the snow flying. Beginners often fail to realize that the duration of a fish's jump is often quite long, and that they needn't release the shutter the moment a fish starts its jump. Try to anticipate how it will jump and anticipate its peak. For a split second the fish will be suspended in the air before crashing back into the water and that's the precise time to release the shutter.

In taking photos of this kind, be alert to anticipate where the fish will jump and hold your camera steady, so that camera movement doesn't spoil the picture.

Action pictures look best when the subject is slightly blurred. Many people who use 35mm cameras make the mistake of taking all action photographs with their shutter set at 1/1000 second. This often freezes the action and the picture looks unnatural. A slower shutter speed—say, 1/500 or 1/250 sec-

Action pictures are enhanced if the subject is slightly blurred to suggest movement, like the wing of this bald eagle. The secret is to use a moderate shutter speed—about 1/250 second—so that the action is not completely stopped.

ond—will often do a better job, because the fish and the water falling away from the fish are blurred, thus giving the feeling of movement. The same holds true of an animal running, or a group of children playing.

WILDLIFE

Photographing animals in their natural habitat can be lots of fun, but it's often quite difficult. If you take your camera and carefully approach animals as they are feeding, playing or resting, you can often obtain fine pictures. Likewise, if you have long telephoto lenses you can also move right in on the animal and obtain excellent closeups.

Telephoto lens is useful but not always necessary for photographing wildlife. Author shot this nest of nutria babies from fishing boat while floating silently along the shore.

Zoom lens set at maximum 220mm focal length caught this turtle sunning on a log. When using a telephoto lens, be sure to hold the camera steady, preferably on a tripod or an improvised rest.

But if you haven't got telephoto lenses you can add an extra dimension to your photography by setting up photographs of this type. Cable release mechanisms, timing devices and trip cords allow you to be far from the game and still get the picture.

The simplest way to get closeups of animals or birds is to set your camera close to an area they're frequenting and then to move away. By knowing just where your camera is focused, you can trip your shutter simply by pressing the cable release many feet from where the animals are being photographed. This technique also works very well when photographing birds. Often they will ignore a camera once it has been in place for a while and you can obtain many fine pictures. Bird feeders are obviously excellent spots for this.

Just recently a shutter release that is activated by a CO_2 cylinder and can be fired over 50 feet away came onto the market, and this no doubt will be useful in outdoor photography when you have difficulty getting close to your subject.

With some types of shutter releases, a simple string can be used to trigger them from a distance. Just make sure that you fasten the camera securely so that it won't move when you pull the string.

One of the simplest ways to get closeup pictures of birds and animals is by using a blind. This can be a natural blind made of materials found near the scene, or it can be a portable blind which you carry with you and erect

Unplanned backlighting, with the sun out of the camera's range, put sparkle into this picture of a nutria waddling through a marsh.

at the site. It may be necessary to leave the blind in place for several days until your subject becomes adjusted to it, but once that happens you are usually home free. By remaining quietly and unobtrusively within the blind, you can photograph the bird or animal to your heart's desire.

It is important to mention that in order to consistently obtain good, crisp pictures you have to keep camera movement to a minimum. Using fast shutter speeds eliminates much of the movement because the lens speed is faster than you may move. But there are times when, because of poor light, you may have to use a slow shutter speed. At such times it is wise to rest your camera on something while releasing the shutter. Better still, use a tripod when you know there will be poor light, or if you're trying to get really crisp shots with a great amount of depth-of-field.

If a tripod isn't readily available, and you're using a telephoto lens, you can always employ a pillow or a rolled-up jacket as a steadying device. Either one works very well, providing a resting spot that will steady the camera and permit you to release the shutter with no movement.

LIGHT AND EXPOSURE

So very much has been written over the years about photography, that very often beginners forget one of the simplest rules: Most of the time, keep the sun behind you when photographing. A bright sun falling on your subject is the best insurance that you'll take a good picture. Side lighting is better at times, and even pointing your camera directly at the sun, with your subject between the camera and the sun, can be very effective.

Shooting directly into the sun usually won't give you the normal type of picture most camera enthusiasts are out for. But it will give you unusual silhouettes that can be extremely rewarding. Early in the morning, with the sun just coming over the horizon, point your camera right into the sun, and take a lens reading of the sun. Position a subject in the foreground, such as an angler casting from the surf, and you'll have a rewarding picture with the angler silhouetted in black, and the sun burning bright, its reflection glistening across the water.

At dusk you can often obtain similar effects, particularly with sunsets, capturing on film the mass of purples, reds and blacks which fill the evening sky. Try various exposures, and you'll be surprised with the varying effects in the finished pictures.

Thanks to today's excellent exposure meters, good cameras and fine-quality films you can depend on most of your pictures being properly exposed if you follow all the instructions. But if you've an opportunity to get an unusual picture and may never again be able to duplicate it, such as a big brown trout you have just landed, or a picturesque waterfall back in the brush, it's wise to use several frames of film and to bracket your exposure by a half stop in either direction, to insure that one of the three or four frames you take will be properly exposed.

Shooting directly into the sun produced dramatic silhouettes in these two photos. Backlighting is most effective in capturing the texture of water.

129

Polaroid camera allows photographer to know immediately whether a photo is satisfactory. If it is not, he merely shoots another.

CANDID SHOTS

One type of picture which always has impact is the photo of someone who doesn't realize he's being photographed. Keep this in mind when you're on a family outing. You don't always have to tell someone you're going to take his picture. Just move in with the camera, compose your picture and release the shutter. Candid shots such as these are often priceless, because they have a genuine quality about them that is often lacking in a posed picture.

SELECTING A CAMERA

Within the wide range of cameras there are four basic types which are well suited for use by the entire family in taking outdoor photographs. They are the picture-in-a-minute types, cartridge-loaded models, twin-lens reflex cameras

Polaroid Colorpack II (left), a low-priced model, takes instant color pictures, has an electronic shutter. Model 360 is a fully automatic camera, with electronic flash, electronic development timer and a sophisticated automatic exposure-control system.

and 35mm cameras. All are capable of producing fine pictures and are available in models at either end of the price spectrum, from economical, easy-to-operate models, on up to costly, sophisticated cameras which are most appropriate for the advanced amateur or semiprofessional.

Polaroid Cameras

For the newcomer to outdoor photography, the Polaroid picture-in-a-minute camera holds a great appeal. It enables him to compose and take a photograph, and know in a minute with color film, and in just seconds with black and white, whether he got a good picture. If he finds that he didn't he can take another one.

Polaroid cameras are available in a wide range of prices, from under $30 for the Colorpack II which has a sharp, three-element lens that produces fine prints, on up to a sophisticated Polaroid 250 which is equipped with a 114mm Tominon lens and has automatic CdS exposure control. You simply load the camera with film, focus with a unique side-to-side focusing system and release the shutter. The result is a perfectly exposed 3¼-by-4¼ print. The fully automatic features of the 250 and Polaroid 180 have made them extremely popular, even though more costly.

The newest Polaroid 360 comes equipped with an electronic flash unit, and even a timer to let you know when the print is ready. It's totally automated and the most modern picture-in-a-minute equipment.

Duplicate negatives are available through Polaroid's copy service, so there's no problem when you want duplicates of that perfect photo.

It should be noted, however, that with a Polaroid camera there is a problem of bulk. It's a big, heavy camera, unwieldy to carry afield. Polaroid cameras produce best results when operated at temperatures of 60 degrees or more, but there is an accessory which may be used when temperatures are lower.

Cartridge-Loaded Cameras

Kodak gave birth to the idea of a cartridge loaded with size 126 film, and thus opened a whole new area of photography to those individuals who like the simplicity of opening the back of a camera, dropping a cartridge into it (instead of loading and threading film) and being ready to take pictures.

The first cartridge-loaded cameras designed for 126 film were essentially cameras for taking snapshots and were ideally suited to the younger generation, who found them easy to load and operate. Priced in the $15 to $25 range they are still very popular, with the Kodak Instamatic commanding by far the greatest popularity. Keep in mind, however, that the Kodak Instamatics are not all snapshot-type cameras, for the Kodak Instamatic 814 has a fast f/2.8 lumenized lens that takes excellent pictures. It sells for $145.

Two types of cartridge-loading cameras: Kodak Instamatic and Instamatic Reflex. The Instamatic has a viewfinder for composing the picture, the Reflex a ground glass. Both have automatic exposure setting and a flashcube socket.

The concept of cartridge loading resulted in several major manufacturers designing single-lens reflex cameras specifically for 126 cartridge-type film. The most notable cameras in this category are the Kodak Instamatic Reflex, Zeiss Contaflex 126 and the Rolleiflex SL26. All are sophisticated cameras that are capable of giving excellent results with 126 film in color or black and white, while using either 12- or 20-exposure cartridges.

The Kodak Instamatic Reflex is available with either a 45mm f/2.8 Xenar lens or a 50mm f/1.9 lens, both of which give fine results. This camera is quite expensive, in the $200-and-up range, depending on the lens you select. It has many fine features, including a battery-powered CdS exposure meter and automatic exposure control. It's light in weight and small in size, which makes it easy to transport afield. There's a minimum of fuss when operating it, too.

One feature of the Instamatic Reflex which makes it more expensive and more versatile is the fact that it will accept interchangeable lenses. In addition to the normal lenses which come with the camera, either the 45mm f/2.8 Xenar lens, or the 50mm f/1.9 Xenon lens, the following accessory lenses are available: a 28mm f/4 lens, a 35mm f/2.8 lens, an 85mm f/4 lens, a 135mm f/4 lens, and a 200mm f/4.8 lens. Closeup lens sets, in addition, which cover a picture-taking range from 38½ to 7 inches, film to subject distance, are available.

Another fine 126 cartridge-loading camera is the Zeiss Contaflex 126, which comes equipped with a 45mm f/2.8 Color-Pantar lens, but has accessory lenses

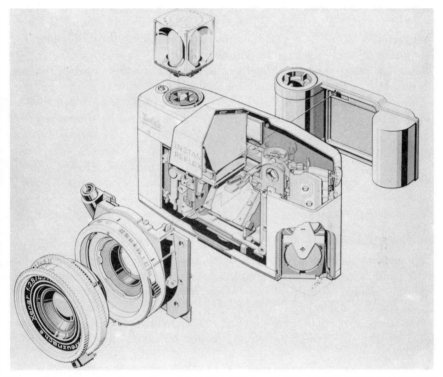

This cutaway drawing shows the relationship of lens, shutter and electronic components in the Instamatic Reflex.

including a 32mm f/2.8 Zeiss Distagon, 85mm f/2.8 Sonnar and a long 135mm f/4 Tele-Tessar. This camera has many fine features, including CdS through-the-lens exposure meter and automatic exposure control. A good camera, built by a manufacturer long known for quality craftsmanship.

Rolleiflex is best known for its twin-lens reflex cameras, but it certainly did a fine job in designing the Rolleiflex SL26, a single-lens reflex camera for 126 cartridge loading. The Rollei comes equipped with an excellent-quality 40mm f/2.8 Zeiss Tessar lens. Its features include a between-the-lens leaf Compur shutter, a through-the-lens CdS meter which measures the full area at full aperture, an instant-return mirror and quick-return diaphragm. It weighs but 20 ounces, is small and compact and perfect for outdoor photography. It has a comfortable rapid-wind film-advance lever and shutter-release mechanism located conveniently right on the top of the camera housing. It's priced at close to $300 but certainly is a fine piece of craftsmanship for the serious photographer who prefers the 126 cartridge-loading type of camera.

Twins-Lens Reflex Cameras

As their name implies, these cameras have twin lenses, one of which is used for viewing and the other for taking the picture. The lenses are mounted vertically, one atop the other, and the subject to be photographed is viewed on a groundglass through the top lens. The image you see on the groundglass is the exact picture you will take, and thus you can compose on the groundglass and know precisely what your results will be.

There are many models of the 2¼-by-2¼ twin-lens reflex cameras, the most notable of which include the Rolleiflex, Rolleicord, Mamiya, Minolta Autocord and the Yashica Mat. They vary greatly in price, from around $40 to $450. This wide range of price is determined, for the most part, by the lower-priced cameras having minimum accessories, and the higher-priced models having automatic shutter cocking when the film is advanced, exposure meters, provisions for taking pictures on either standard 120 film with 12 exposures, or 220 film with 24 exposures, or even standard 35mm film. Some have self-timers for taking your own pictures. Naturally, the cameras equipped with fine-quality lenses cost more.

The 35mm Cameras

The most popular 35mm cameras today are reflex models with a focal-plane shutter and rangefinder models, although the former are more numerous. In a 35mm camera, as with other cameras, you get what you pay for. There are economy-priced models of many 35s available, but these are equipped with so few features that often it is wiser to stick with an economical Instamatic model than to move into an economy 35mm, for you'll usually obtain better results.

It's wise to give serious thought to obtaining a good-quality, moderate-priced 35mm camera. Once you have a camera with a good body, shutter and built-in exposure meter, you can always add accessories when you are ready. With economy-priced cameras this isn't always possible.

Germany and Japan each share the spotlight in building top-quality 35mm rangefinder cameras. The Canon 7S is the finest in the line of excellent cameras by the Canon Camera Company of Tokyo and sells for approximately $325, when equipped with a 50mm f/1.4 Canon lens. It is equipped with a metal focal-plane shutter with speeds ranging from 1 to 1/1000 second. The camera has a bright frame viewfinder with a coupled rangefinder. It has many other quality features, including a CdS exposure meter coupled to the shutter control for films with a speed to ASA 400.

From Germany comes the Leica 35mm rangefinder camera. The Leica M4 is an expensive camera, costing approximately $500 when equipped with a

50mm Summilux lens, but it is a camera that has many devotees throughout the world who swear by its dependability and versatility. It has a focal-plane shutter with speeds from 1 to 1/1000 second and has a combined rangefinder-viewfinder, with parallax-correcting projected frames for 35mm, 50mm, 90mm, and 135mm lenses.

The major manufacturers of 35mm reflex cameras with focal-plane shutters are also located in Germany and Japan. Because there is such great similarity among most 35mm SLR cameras, it would be repetitious to discuss each camera's features. It becomes a matter of the buyer carefully evaluating each of the camera's features and determining if the particular model he is interested in will do the job he wants it to do.

The 35mm cameras are ideally suited to outdoor photography because they are small in size, usually 5 to 6 inches in length, less than 3¾ inches from front to back and about of equal height. Most weigh around two pounds, plus or minus a couple of ounces, which means they're not too cumbersome to hang around your neck, or to slip into the pocket of a hunting jacket when traveling afield.

Most of these cameras have shutters with speeds from 1 to 1/1000 second, plus B, FP, and X synchronization. Many have a self-timer.

They have a variety of film-advance mechanisms, although the film-advance lever on the top of the camera appears to be the most popular because of the speed and ease with which you can advance film and shoot. Most have either an interchangeable or noninterchangeable eye-level prism with a full focusing screen. Some have a split-image rangefinder.

Most models are equipped with battery-powered CdS exposure meters, behind the lens, which measure the entire picture area at shooting aperture, although some have behind-the-lens exposure meters which measure a central spot at full aperture. Other features of the cameras mentioned here include instant-return mirror, quick-return diaphragm, depth-of-field preview buttons and film-type reminders.

FLASH EQUIPMENT

There are times, however, indoors or perhaps outdoors at night, when illumination can add impact to your photographs. At that time flash illumination is most often used by photographers, who employ either flashbulbs, flash cubes or electronic flash for their light source.

Years ago almost everyone used flashbulbs. But because of their inconvenience, bulk and cost they have lost favor in recent years to the modern flash cube, which may be used with an adapter on most cameras. You simply snap the cube into the camera, and you can take a total of four photographs, the cube automatically turning after you take each picture.

Another popular item is electronic flash. Because of transistors and modern circuitry, the modern electronic flash unit used on most amateur cameras has been reduced in size until it is as small as a pack of cigarettes, and in some cases smaller! There are almost as many manufacturers and models of electronic flash as there are 35mm cameras, and the majority of their units do a serviceable job of illuminating the picture area. As with most camera equipment, it is important that you investigate the various models available and select one which will best suit your needs. As an amateur you probably won't require a big, heavy-duty unit like those used by professionals. This limits you to units capable of delivering fewer flashes per shooting session, but it also saves you a substantial amount of money.

Electronic flash units are, in many instances, made to be used with specific types of cameras. Polaroid has an automatic electronic flash unit which attaches to its new Polaroid 360 camera. It has nickel-cadmium rechargeable batteries that may be fully charged in just an hour by plugging into house current. Thus you always have a flash ready to use, and at no additional cost.

With 126 cartridge-loaded cameras in the economy models the flash cube continues to be the most popular source of illumination, although on the better-quality 126 cameras many photographers use electronic flash units.

Electronic flash units, or strobes as they have come to be known, are very popular with the users of twin-lens reflex cameras and 35mm cameras. The Honeywell Auto/Strobonar 660 and 600, which sell at approximately $150 and $90, are favored by many serious photographers. The model 660 is fully automatic, delivering the proper light output for the film being used in the camera, while the model 600 delivers a constant amount of light.

Many 35mm camera users find the Strobonar 400 to their liking. It sells for approximately $70, and operates on much the same principle as the model 600.

Among the popular electronic flash units are the Braun, Ultrablitz, Kako, Mecablitz and Heliotron. Today almost all are equipped with rechargeable nickel-cadmium batteries and have high guide-number ratings. It is important to select a unit that will not fire until it is fully charged, so that you get the peak power of the unit. Look for a unit having a quick recycling time—the time between flashes—which can be important in the outdoors when you're attempting to take a series of sequence-type pictures, such as fighting a fish.

While many people think of using flash only in poor light conditions or at night, it also proves extremely useful during the daytime, particularly in bright sun. Often an extremely bright sun will make harsh, black shadows across a person's face when he is wearing a hat. The sun will also cause dark shadows in the cockpit of a boat. Flash cubes and electronic flash may be effectively used to eliminate these harsh shadows when used as secondary light, or flash fill. The flash simply reaches in and fills up the shadows, illuminating them just enough so that there is even lighting throughout. Often the use of flash fill will give that professional touch to an otherwise dull photograph.

FILM

You'll find there are many types of film available, each of which is designed for a specific purpose. In color film there is negative color, which is used for color prints, and positive color, which is used for transparencies. There are fast color films, which give what are often called "cold" or true-to-life colors, and there are slow color films, which give "warm" colorful pictures that lean heavily towards bright reds and yellows.

In black and white films there are extremely fine-grain films which are somewhat slow in speed, and extremely fast films that do not have as good contrast, but get the picture in even poor light conditions.

Kodak film is without a doubt the most popular brand of film used by camera enthusiasts in America today, but many enjoy fine results while using Dynachrome, Agfachrome and Anscochrome films. In the final analysis it's a matter of personal preference, depending on what types of pictures you'll be taking—still life or action, color or black and white—and whether you want prints or wish to view transparencies.

CARE OF CAMERA AND FILM

In the outdoors cameras and camera equipment are exposed to the elements. Heat, humidity, dust, salt spray and water can play havoc with all equipment. So care should always be exercised to protect the equipment from the elements whenever possible. If the equipment is accidentally wet during a shower, make every attempt to dry it thoroughly, and to store it in something other than an airtight case until everything is thoroughly dried. Keep your lenses free of dirt and grime by using a small camel's-hair brush and lens tissue. Use a soft cloth on the camera body to keep it free of dirt and grime which can and will accumulate no matter how careful you are, especially when using the camera in the outdoors.

Never, but never, leave your cameras or film in direct sun. The sun can physically damage a camera, especially in warm climates where there is intense heat generated within the camera body. When traveling, never make the mistake of transporting your camera or camera equipment in the trunk of your car unless it is well insulated. The trunk can become extremely hot and may not only damage your camera equipment, but your film as well. Keep the camera inside the car where the temperature is cooler and there is more ventilation.

The glove compartment of an automobile can also be a death trap for cameras, and especially for film. Don't put your camera in the glove compartment.

There are two simple items familiar to all sportsmen which serve extremely well in protecting cameras and camera equipment from the outdoor elements. One is the plastic bag, and the other is the styrofoam chest.

The heavy plastic transparent bags available in all grocery stores are great for protecting cameras and film from dust, dirt and dampness. Simply slip one over your camera and fasten it with a rubberband. Protect your film in the same way; then, if it accidentally gets a dunking, you haven't lost anything.

Styrofoam chests are inexpensive and come in a wide variety of shapes and sizes. They provide superb insulation from both cold and heat for cameras and film, and are extremely useful for carrying cameras in an automobile or boat.

I have an expensive leather camera case which is very professional looking and very useful, but which does not protect either cameras or film from the heat. One of my favorite tricks is to place this entire camera bag inside a large styrofoam chest in the trunk of my car. I sometimes do the same thing in a boat, and have the confident assurance that my precious equipment and film are fully protected.

Another "camera case" which serves me especially well on fishing and boating trips for protection from severe heat is one which I have made from a converted Plano tackle box. With the trays removed, this waterproof box makes a safe, protected, inconspicuous container for my cameras while afloat. With the top of the box open, the cameras and equipment are immediately available for use, yet at the first threat of rain I can close the top and my equipment is secure.

Another excellent case used by many professionals is the aluminum case made by Halliburton. Originally made as suitcases, and still used for this purpose, these are now available in models designed especially for camera use. They are expensive, but are dustproof, extremely strong and will last for years. When properly padded with foam insulation, they protect camera and lenses from surprisingly severe shocks.

One of the mistakes which the majority of amateur photographers in this country makes is to leave a roll of partially exposed film in the camera for weeks or months before having it developed. When you return from an outing and have a few exposures left on a roll, go ahead and use them and have the film processed. It is much better to have the film processed and lose a few exposures which you don't take than to leave it in the camera for weeks and lose the entire roll. Not only are you losing a roll of film, but you are losing the images of that recreational outing which you recorded.

9 Winter Activities

WINTER IS a period of the year which means many things to many people, depending largely upon the part of the country where they live. Until about ten years ago, however, for most sportsmen the advent of winter meant a virtual end to their outdoor activities.

Naturally, some of the outdoor activities we enjoy during the summertime are not suitable for cold weather, but it is amazing how many suddenly become possible and pleasurable once the sportsman's mental block is removed. When the temperature gets low, I lose all interest in swimming, but that same bite in the air makes a cookout even more inviting.

During the winter months the majority of people can expect severely cold weather. But there are few areas where the weather does not change substantially, even during the depths of winter, between cold snaps and periods of moderation. If you are prepared both mentally and physically, you can take advantage of these fine conditions. Even during periods when winter temperatures drop to freezing and below, sportsmen who keep their families by the hearth are denying them many weeks of outdoor pleasure.

Winter fishing is frequently excellent, yet most lakes and streams are lonesome places when the temperatures begin to slide. In a great part of the country, fishing is permitted year-round, especially for the warm-water species such as bass, bluegills and crappie.

When young Eddie Simerell established the first world record for spotted bass, an event which took place on Smith Lake in Alabama about four years ago, the temperature on that biting cold day was about 15 degrees. On that same day, Eddie and his dad caught a string of bass, including the 7-pound lunker which topped all previous spotted bass ever taken, that would have warmed the heart of any angler.

One of the largest limit strings of fifteen bass ever taken in my area, a string which averaged 5 pounds, was caught on a bleak February day with

Ice fishing for bass, bluegills and crappie is permitted in most states, and the catches often surpass those made by the summer angler.

the temperature shivering at the 18-degree mark. They were caught by a sportsman who hadn't been told that fishing was supposed to be a warm-weather sport.

Winter fishing frequently can be pleasanter than summer fishing. It's sometimes much easier to cope with cold weather, by putting on the proper clothing, than it is to cope with the searing heat of midsummer.

In most areas of the country wintertime is the off season, and rates at lodges, clubs and campgrounds are correspondingly reduced. Campgrounds which are overloaded in July and August go begging for customers when December, January and February roll around.

Snow-covered hills pose a perennial challenge to skiers and sledders.

141

The old and the new confront each other in a winter setting. Speeding cross-country at 35 mph, snowmobile leaves horse and sleigh to the well-traveled road—and history.

There are many fringe benefits to the cold-weather period. A big bonfire—roasting wieners or marshmallows—is a great treat for children and adults. When the temperatures start to slide, cooking outdoors in cool to cold weather, while camping or just on a cookout, is more comfortable than it is during the hot summertime. And big pots of stew or spaghetti and beans have a particular attraction when their aroma is wafted about on a cold breeze.

In many parts of the country, hiking is much easier in the wintertime because heavy vegetation has been killed by frosts. It's my wife's favorite time of the year for gathering dried materials such as seed pods, because the foliage is down.

Boating can be winter fun, in areas where lakes do not freeze over, but there are special precautions to be observed. Keep in mind that the effect of cold is multiplied many times if you are moving rapidly.

As an example, let's assume that the air temperature is just below freezing, say 30 degrees. If you are in an open boat, exposed to wind traveling at a speed of 30 miles per hour, the chilling effect on your body is equivalent to a temperature of −2 degrees in still air. It's obvious that you and your family would need much greater protection from the elements under such conditions than would at first seem necessary.

The temperature doesn't have to be frightfully cold in fact for this chill factor to have its effect. The sportsman who is boating, or fishing from a boat, should keep this in mind at all seasons of the year, and dress himself and his family accordingly.

This wind-chill rating, let me emphasize, is just as important whether it's created by blowing wind or by your own movement, or by a combination of both. As any sportsman already knows, it just seems colder than the thermometer actually is when the wind is blowing. Dress yourself and your family accordingly.

WINTER CLOTHING

The key to the enjoyment of the outdoors during cold weather lies in using suitable clothing. I am constantly amazed at the vast number of sportsmen who seem unaware that there are items of clothing available—jackets, pants, underwear, boots, caps—which are far superior to anything they actually use. Even the very best is only slightly more expensive than the mediocre and, like the cost of other quality outdoor gear, it is moderate when prorated over the life of the item.

Perhaps you are hardy enough, veteran outdoorsman, to cope with the winter elements with a minimum of clothing, but don't make the mistake of trying to stint when you buy winter clothing for your wife and youngsters. Outdoor recreation can be great during cold weather, but it can also be miserable for those who go afield ill clad.

One thing to keep in mind when acquiring winter clothing for your family is to keep it as light in weight as possible. If they are burdened with heavy gear, the effort of simply moving around in the outdoors will prove to be exhausting in a short time, and this is so unnecessary with the availability of the excellent lightweight clothing now on the market.

Boots designed for snowmobiling are warm and waterproof.

There are quite a number of mail-order houses, as well as individual retail stores, where excellent winter clothing is available, and some of them have been mentioned earlier in this book. I refer again to the Seattle-based firm of Eddie Bauer, Inc., 417 East Pine Street, Seattle, Washington. This is a mail-order firm and a catalog is available, free for the asking.

Snowmobile suits come in all sizes and keep even the smallest ice fisherman warm.

The Eddie Bauer Company, now under the management of Bill Niemi and his son, is an institution among outdoorsmen. The quality of the down garments and sleeping bags made by Bauer for years is legendary, and the question, "Is that a Bauer coat?" has the same connotation that the question, "Is that a Stradivarius?" has to a violinist. Most of the Arctic and Polar expeditions, and most of the assaults on such mountain peaks as Mt. Everest, have been outfitted with down gear by Bauer.

The company features clothing for women and youngsters, as do some other firms throughout the country, which is not only sufficient in combating winter cold, but is attractive as well. It is smartly styled and colorful, and keep in mind that this is important to the ladies.

Although it is true that a great portion of the United States does not have

Winter water skiing has its hardy advocates—but be sure to wear a waterproof suit.

snow during most of the wintertime, it is also very true that when most of us think of winter sports we think of those associated with snow. Up until a decade ago the focus of winter sports always centered on the ski resort areas of the northeast and in such western resorts as Sun Valley, Aspen and Vail. "Winter sports" was snow skiing and ice skating and ice fishing. All that has changed.

Not that these resorts aren't still in business, or that snow skiing has lost any of its appeal, but something new has been added.

SNOWMOBILING

It was just ten years ago that a critter called the Ski-Doo sidled down into the United States from Canada, and it proved to be the biggest sleeper in the outdoor field in decades. The Ski-Doo was a snowmobile, a vehicle which superficially resembles a motorcycle and which is propelled by a tank-type track or two. That year Bombardier, Ltd., manufacturer of the Ski-Doo, sold 225 machines in the United States. There were probably not more than 4,000 snowmobiles being produced each year by a handful of manufacturers, but what a difference a decade has made.

There are now more than fifty manufacturers producing snowmobiles, and they sell more than a quarter of a million of these machines each year. Bombardier alone sold more than 114,000 Ski-Doos in 1969.

There are many reasons for the popularity of these vehicles. They have emancipated northern families during the frigid snow-covered winter months. They have opened up a whole new array of activities which were virtually beyond reach prior to the advent of snowmobiles. In the northern part of this country and in the mountainous areas of the West, summer cottages were forgotten when the snow hit, since they are usually far from the snowplowed highways, but now they've become the center of activities for many families throughout the year. Hunters use the machines to get into remote areas; game wardens and law enforcement officials have added mobility; farmers use them to haul food to livestock; fishermen zip out on the ice of lakes in snowmobiles.

The fact is that simply riding a snowmobile is fun. They will carry one or two people, and will breeze along effortlessly at 35 or 40 miles per hour. The racing models will even hit speeds of 70 miles per hour and more. Snowmobiles cost from $500 to $1500, and are transported from home to the snow area on a trailer just like a boat. In most of the snow-belt areas of the nation, the snowmobile has become as much of a status symbol as a boat, and two-snowmobile families and three-snowmobile families are not at all unusual.

Thermal clothing has been developed so that you stay warm yet do not perspire and catch cold. Clothing, in many cases, matches the color of the snow machine, as vehicle manufacturers either own their own clothing operations or license established manufacturers to make clothing for them. The company trademark is on the suits, the name of the club the family belongs to, and maybe a whole sleeve or two is filled with patches showing races, rallies, and snow events the family has attended.

Thermal boots are also necessary. The best have a nylon outer shell with inner felt boot liners and heavy rubber soles. This doesn't sound like much in below-zero weather, but the trick to enjoying being outdoors for any length of time is to prevent excess perspiration. Perspiration will freeze, so snowmobile clothing breathes, and the wearer is comfortable.

Hats, wool or hard, some fitted with helmet liners, and special gloves with big clips so they can be attached together and onto your belt or machine handlebars to prevent losing them, are also important. Face masks, goggles and scarfs, some done up in the best psychedelic fashion, add to the color of a rally or family cruise.

Snowmobilers trailer their machines to lake cottages, formerly abandoned in the winter-time, and enjoy this fast-growing sport. Special cover protects the snowmobile in transit.

It's sufficient to say that no recreational snowmobiler should buy a machine without also discussing clothing. It's an added expense, but just as important as buying a good life jacket.

It is wise to have a simple repair kit aboard a machine. Vehicles are now being made with adequate storage compartments. Extra gas in clean plastic soap bottles is a necessity. Be sure you label the bottles. Another necessity is a spark-plug wrench, along with extra spark plugs. Snowmobile engines are similar to your outboard or lawnmower. Gas must be pre-mixed with oil before pouring it into the gas tank. Improper mixture fouls plugs, and with cold weather liable to set up another starting blockage, it is much simpler to be ready with extra plugs.

In case of a complete breakdown, wise snowmobilers are now carrying the new fiberglass snowshoes with them. This is sensible. If the machine gets completely bogged down in deep powder snow, only snowshoes will carry a person out of the wilderness with any chance of survival.

Some snow fans overload machines with supplies they laughingly call their disaster kits, just as many boats are overloaded. However, in addition to the gear mentioned above, flares, a small squirt can full of gas, matches, a flashlight, some dried foods which can be mixed with snow, a first-aid kit and a small gas fire stove are good things to carry.

The best flotation is achieved with the proper snow base and compatible density. This doesn't mean much to the average user at this time because the sport has grown so fast in such a short time that it is difficult to get persons off the machines when any snow condition exists. They're operable over most terrain and cover. Experienced snowmobilers are even driving their machines on wetted-down grass in the snow states, and over the dunes and sand in other states. Wheel conversion kits for front skis are available.

The first-time rider should be cautious. The machine floats on snow as a boat floats on water. It is driven like a motorcycle—you lean with it. If you lean the wrong way, you or the machine could hit a tree, a stump or a rock. Anybody old enough to drive a bicycle can pilot a snowmobile safely. Just acquire a feel for the machine, as an experienced boatman does for a boat.

Snowmobile clubs have formed all over the snow belt. The clubs sponsor weekend races and trips, and have pressed for the development of trails.

Unless there is an actual mechanical defect, about the most serious thing to watch for is a frozen throttle, or perhaps frozen brake controls. Linkage between the right-hand throttle and the engine, and the left-hand brake calipers and the drive train, sometimes gets encrusted with snow or ice. It will melt under lights, heat lamps or sun while parked outside. Any water or snow accumulating will freeze rapidly once on a trail again, and machine handling could become difficult.

Trailering a machine is like trailering a boat. Winter poses its particular problems for good trailering. Tie-downs become doubly important because cold can snap buckles, ropes and connections.

The best part of traveling to a snow area, especially from a city in a snow state, is that traffic is diminished compared to ordinary summer travel. Not only that, most roads—except during the time of a snowstorm—are much cleaner and safer. You often see wildlife; the snow blankets the countryside; and, when the bright sun comes out, the scenery is beautiful.

Once you reach a snow area, there are many things to do. There's probably a good race going on over the weekend somewhere nearby. There are miles and miles of trails through county, state and federal forests. This is especially true in Wisconsin, Michigan and Minnesota, and in most snow-belt states. The midwestern states do seem to have the edge on snowmobile trail development. Trails have standard markers in the forest so that you cannot get lost; they often lead to public or private roadside restaurants, taverns and warming places. Many county and village people provide a constable or volunteer local snow club to "sweep" the trails when dusk approaches to check on stragglers or breakdowns. It is a good idea to register with somebody if traveling alone, and it is a better idea never to travel alone. Snowmobiling is safer, more secure, and more enjoyable when individuals team up on trails.

Information about trails, parking areas and other facilities can generally be obtained at any county agent office. Local Chambers of Commerce also have this information.

A natural growth of the great family interest in snowmobiling is the formation of snowmobile clubs. Most clubs are organized by local groups, sometimes to sponsor weekend races and rallies which promote their towns and their snowmobile facilities; but more often, to enjoy this new sport safely. They also have been instrumental in the development of trails, and in preventing legislation which would be adverse to the activity.

Such legislation comes up because, as in any sport, snowmobiling has its renegades. These people are no different than the poachers, deer shiners, fish trappers and other unsavory people who invade all recreational domains to the detriment of the law abiders.

Surprisingly enough, there is a great deal more of this kind of trouble in the backwoods areas than there is in urban areas where parks are available. City people must conform, especially when they're in the city.

In the North, the snowmobile has opened up trespassing on private property and subsequent looting of private summer homes. Deputies are now equipped with snowmobiles and hopefully they're as fast as those of the lawbreakers.

One very real hazard of snowmobiling in some areas is the possibility of hitting single strands of wire, which are difficult to see if you are moving very fast. Such an accident can cause serious injury or even death, so be extremely cautious when traveling over unfamiliar terrain.

Believe it or not, there have been cases of stolen snowmobiles. Owners have had them taken off the rear of their cars and driven away, trailer and all. Use the same kind of precautions which you would with a trailered boat.

Expert racers from all over the country compete each year in world snowmobile championships at Eagle River, Wisconsin. Here Steve Ave, of Duluth, Minnesota, three-time winner, puts a 40-hp Ski-Doo T'NT through its paces as he passes a rival on a curve.

The actual north country, while having its great trails, does not have the parks and wide-open spaces found near cities. This means that snowmobile owners can't take their machines on a trailer to a park (there are a few exceptions), and many just drive along the shoulder of a highway to reach their destination. In some states, this is against the law, and it is often very dangerous.

Hunters and fishermen find snowmobiles helpful. Ice fishing is popular in snow country, although not all counties allow the machines on ice unless they can carry flotation equipment. Such devices have been made, but they are not popular with fishermen. Deer hunters use snowmobiles for bringing out a kill. They cannot, however, carry a loaded gun on a machine, nor can they shoot from it.

Wardens, trappers, even doctors on emergency calls, fire and police departments, rangers and farmers all have found uses for the machine. There's no doubt that it has opened up snow country.

Snowmobiles can soon be fitted with an ambulance sled to remove injured skiers from slopes, or perhaps transport a mother-to-be to a hospital. Public-service companies are testing the machine with a trailer fitted out with equipment and tools, enabling them to get back off the road following severe storms.

Manufacturers have been enthusiastic about the tremendous acceptance of the snow machines. They are also doing their best to make the sport safer and more acceptable. One sponsors a safety code for adoption by clubs. Another offers moonlight safaris at the major derbies. Others offer booklets on how to organize snow clubs or snowmobile rallies.

More than fifty manufacturers are now members of the International Snowmobile Industries Association. The Association is dedicated to the development of the sport as a family activity.

Snowmobile rental package tours are now available from many resorts and Chambers of Commerce. They are promoted and publicized in such cities as Chicago, Denver, Milwaukee, Indianapolis and St. Louis. Most include bus transportation, meals (including trail cookouts), lodging, one snow machine for every two persons and a trail guide for a three-day weekend. This type of snowmobiling recreation will certainly grow.

The snowmobile has given camping an additional boost. People now go camping in winter. They actually camp in their campers and in tents, at state and county parks and in national parks and forests, because they can enjoy the area around them via snowmobile.

In metropolitan areas, city people who never see the deep woods can snowmobile. Milwaukee is a case in point, as it was the first major city in the nation to open up the golf courses and parks of its outstanding park system to snowmobiles.

The county park commission rented machines and also sold season permits for park use to machine owners. When there was enough snow cover, the rental business was terrific.

There is rental in resort areas, too, for those who do not own machines. Vacationers using rental machines often turn into fans, and the next time they often arrive pulling their own machines.

All in all, the machine has made an impressive impact on snow areas. It has opened up areas which formerly closed down completely because skiing and other winter recreational facilities were not available.

It has drawn the attention of the national and overseas press because it is so new, and because the sport of racing is so competitive it provides a great spectator sport.

More important, it provides a perfect outlet for a winter vacation for the entire family. The machine has made ice fishing, hunting and camping more popular than ever before.

INDEX